The Collected Works of
James M. Buchanan

VOLUME 8
Democracy in Deficit

James M. Buchanan and Richard E. Wagner,
Big Sky, Montana

The Collected Works of

James M. Buchanan

VOLUME 8

Democracy in Deficit

The Political Legacy of Lord Keynes

James M. Buchanan and
Richard E. Wagner

LIBERTY FUND

Indianapolis

This book is published by Liberty Fund, Inc., a foundation
established to encourage study of the ideal of a society of free
and responsible individuals.

𒀀𒈫

The cuneiform inscription that serves as our logo and as the design
motif for our endpapers is the earliest-known written appearance
of the word "freedom" (*amagi*), or "liberty." It is taken from a clay
document written about 2300 B.C. in the Sumerian city-state of Lagash.

| 04 | 03 | 02 | 01 | 00 | C | 5 | 4 | 3 | 2 | 1 |
| 04 | 03 | 02 | 01 | 00 | P | 5 | 4 | 3 | 2 | 1 |

Library of Congress Cataloging-in-Publication Data
Buchanan, James M.
Democracy in deficit : the political legacy of Lord Keynes / James M. Buchanan and
Richard E. Wagner.
p. cm. — (The collected works of James M. Buchanan ; v. 8)
Originally published : New York : Academic Press. c1977. With a
new foreword.
Includes bibliographical references and index.
ISBN 0-86597-227-3 (hc : alk. paper). — ISBN 0-86597-228-1 (pbk : alk. paper)
1. United States—Economic policy. 2. Fiscal policy—United
States. 3. Keynesian economics. I. Wagner, Richard E. II.
Title. III. Series: Buchanan, James M. Works. 1999 ; v. 8.
HC106.6.B74 2000
330.973'09—dc21 99-24064

LIBERTY FUND, INC.
8335 Allison Pointe Trail, Suite 300
Indianapolis, IN 46250-1684

Contents

Foreword

Democracy in Deficit, by James M. Buchanan and Richard E. Wagner, represents one of the first comprehensive attempts to apply the basic principles of public choice analysis to macroeconomic theory and policy.[1] Until the 1970s, macroeconomics was devoid of any behavioral content with respect to its treatment of government. Government was simply treated as an exogenous force ($\overline{G}$), which behaved in the way prescribed by a given macroeconomic theory. In this approach, government invariably acted in the public interest as perceived by the host theory. Both the so-called Keynesian and monetarist approaches were beset by this problem, although it was the inherent contradictions of the Keynesian theory that attracted the attention of Buchanan and Wagner.

Democracy in Deficit led the way in economics in endogenizing the role of government in discussions of macroeconomic theory and policy. The central purpose of the book was to examine the simple precepts of Keynesian economics through the lens of public choice theory. The basic discovery was that Keynesian economics had a bias toward deficits in terms of political self-interest. That is, at the margin politicians preferred easy choices to hard ones, and this meant lower taxes and higher spending. Thus, whatever the merits of Keynesian economics in using government fiscal policy to "balance" the forces of inflation and deflation and employment and unemployment in an economy, its application in a democratic setting had severe problems of incentive compatibility; that is, there was a bias toward deficit finance. And, of course, there is no need to reiterate here the evidence in the United States

---

1. James M. Buchanan and Richard E. Wagner, *Democracy in Deficit: The Political Legacy of Lord Keynes* (New York: Academic Press, 1977), volume 8 in the series.

and elsewhere for the correctness of the Buchanan insight on Keynesian economics. It is all too apparent that the thesis of this book has been borne out.

Democracy in Deficit led the way to modern work on political business cycles and the incorporation of public choice considerations into macroeconomic theory. For example, there is a literature today that discusses the issue of the time consistency of economic policy. Does a conservative incumbent who cannot stand for reelection run a deficit in order to control spending by a liberal successor? One can easily see the hand of Buchanan in such constructions. In this example, term limits (a public choice phenomenon) are at the center of a macroeconomic model.

Moreover, monetarism has not escaped the inspection of public choice analysis. Buchanan and others have pioneered work on the behavior of fiat money monopolists. This public choice work stands in stark contrast to earlier work by Keynesians and monetarists who supposed that economists stood outside and above politics and offered advice to politicians and central banks that would be automatically adopted. Otherwise, policymakers were misguided or uninformed. If they knew the right thing, they would do the right thing. This approach to macroeconomics is now largely dead, thanks to books like *Democracy in Deficit*. Today, the age-old adage that incentives matter is heeded by macroeconomists, and it is recognized that political incentive—not the ivory tower advice of economists—drives macroeconomic events.

Democracy in Deficit is also closely related to Buchanan's interest in fiscal and monetary rules to guide long-run policy in macroeconomics. Such rules are needed to overcome the short-run political incentives analyzed in this book and to provide a stable basis for long-run economic growth. Buchanan's lifelong dedication to the goal of a balanced budget amendment to the United States Constitution and to a regime of monetary rules rather than central bank discretion can be seen in this light.

The real alternative to fiscal and monetary rules is, after all, not the perfection of economic policy in some economic theorist's dream. It is what the rough and tumble of ordinary politics produces. The problem is to find a feasible solution to long-run economic stability and growth. Viewed in this way, there is really no conflict between rules and discretion, and, thanks in part to Buchanan's insistence on this point, the world today seems poised to have more rule-based economic institutions. *Democracy in Deficit* is but one of Buchanan's many intellectual efforts toward this end.

Robert D. Tollison
University of Mississippi
1998

Richard E. Wagner

The analytical core of the argument in *Democracy in Deficit* is simple and straightforward. Indeed, the argument is perhaps the single most persuasive application of the elementary theory of public choice, which focuses primary attention on the incentives faced by choosers in varying social roles.

Richard Wagner and I did not sense any purpose of the book beyond that of laying out the elementary propositions along with the implications. Wagner, as colleague and coauthor, was helpful in placing the concept into its history-of-ideas context, and in his continued insistence that even the simplest arguments must be elaborated to be convincing to skeptics.

Neither Dick Wagner nor I suffer fools gladly, but without our mutually enforcing constraints, a book by either of us would have surely lapsed too readily into polemics.

James M. Buchanan
Fairfax, Virginia
1998

Preface

The *economics* of Keynes has been exhaustively discussed, in the popular press, in elementary textbooks, and in learned treatises. By contrast, the *politics* of Keynes and Keynesianism has been treated sketchily and indirectly, if at all. This is surprising, especially in the light of accumulating evidence that tends to support the hypotheses that may be derived from elementary analysis. Our purpose is to fill this void, at least to the extent of initiating a dialogue. We shall advance our argument boldly, in part because our central objective is to introduce a different aspect of Keynesianism for critical analysis. Those who feel obligated to respond to our prescriptive diagnosis of economic-political reality must do so by taking into account elements that have hitherto been left unexamined.

The book is concerned, firstly, with the impact of economic ideas on political institutions, and, secondly, with the effects of these derived institutional changes on economic policy decisions. This approach must be distinguished from that which describes orthodox normative economics. In the latter, the economist provides policy advice and counsel in terms of preferred or optimal results. He does not bother with the transmission of this counsel through the processes of political choice. Nor does he consider the potential influence that his normative suggestions may exert on the basic institutions of politics and, through this influence, in turn, on the results that are generated. To the extent that observed events force him to acknowledge some such influence of ideas on institutions, and of institutions on ideas, the orthodox economist is ready to fault the public and the politicians for failures to cut through the institutional haze. Whether they do so or not, members of the public "should" see the world as the economist sees it.

We reject this set of blindfolds. We step back one stage, and we try to observe the political along with the economic process. We look at the *political economy.* The prescriptive diagnosis that emerges suggests disease in the political structure as it responds to the Keynesian teachings about economic policy. Our specific hypothesis is that the Keynesian theory of economic policy produces inherent biases when applied within the institutions of political democracy. To the extent that this hypothesis is accepted, the search for improvement must be centered on modification in the institutional structure. We cannot readily offer new advice to politicians while at the same time offering predictions as to how these same politicians will behave under existing institutional constraints. By necessity, we must develop a positive theory of how politics works, of public choice, before we can begin to make suggestions for institutional reform.

In our considered judgment, the historical record corroborates the elementary hypotheses that emerge from our analysis. For this reason, we have found it convenient to organize the first part of this book as a history of how ideas developed and exerted their influence on institutions. We should emphasize, however, that the acceptability of our basic analysis does not require that the fiscal record be interpreted in our terms. Those whose natural bent is more Panglossian may explain the observed record differently, while at the same time acknowledging that our analysis does isolate biases in the fiscal decision processes, biases which, in this view, would remain more potential than real.

Some may interpret our argument to be unduly alarmist. We hope that events will prove them right. As noted, we are pessimistic about both the direction and the speed of change. But we are not fatalists. This book is written in our faith in the ability of Americans to shape their own destiny. We hope that the consequences predicted by the logic of our argument will not, in fact, occur, that our conditional predictions will be refuted, and that institutions will be changed. Indeed, we should like to consider this book to be an early part of a dialogue that will result indirectly in the destruction of its more positive arguments. We offer our thoughts on Keynesianism and the survival of democratic values in the hope that our successors a century hence will look on the middle years of the twentieth century as an episodic and dangerous detour away from the basic stability that must be a necessary element in the American dream itself.

Our analysis is limited to the impact of Keynesian ideas on the United States structure of political decision making. The "political legacy" in our

PART ONE

What Happened?

1. What Hath Keynes Wrought?

In the year (1776) of the American Declaration of Independence, Adam Smith observed that "What is prudence in the conduct of every private family, can scarce be folly in that of a great kingdom." Until the advent of the "Keynesian revolution" in the middle years of this century, the fiscal conduct of the American Republic was informed by this Smithian principle of fiscal responsibility: Government should not spend without imposing taxes; and government should not place future generations in bondage by deficit financing of public outlays designed to provide temporary and short-lived benefits.

With the completion of the Keynesian revolution, these time-tested principles of fiscal responsibility were consigned to the heap of superstitious nostrums that once stifled enlightened political-fiscal activism. Keynesianism stood the Smithian analogy on its head. The stress was placed on the differences rather than the similarities between a family and the state, and notably with respect to principles of prudent fiscal conduct. The state was no longer to be conceived in the image of the family, and the rules of prudent fiscal conduct differed dramatically as between the two institutions. The message of Keynesianism might be summarized as: What is folly in the conduct of a private family may be prudence in the conduct of the affairs of a great nation.

"We are all Keynesians now." This was a familiar statement in the 1960s, attributed even to the likes of Milton Friedman among the academicians and to Richard Nixon among the politicians. Yet it takes no scientific talent to observe that ours is not an economic paradise. During the post-Keynesian, post-1960 era, we have labored under continuing and increasing budget deficits, a rapidly growing governmental sector, high unemployment, apparently permanent and perhaps increasing inflation, and accompanying disenchantment with the American sociopolitical order.

This is not as it was supposed to be. After Walter Heller's finest hours in 1963, fiscal wisdom was to have finally triumphed over fiscal folly. The national economy was to have settled down on or near its steady growth potential, onward and upward toward better things, public and private. The spirit of optimism was indeed contagious, so much so that economic productivity and growth, the announced objectives for the post-Sputnik, post-Eisenhower years, were soon abandoned, to be replaced by the redistributionist zeal of Lyndon Johnson's "Great Society" and by the no-growth implications of Ralph Nader, the Sierra Club, Common Cause, and Edmund Muskie's Environmental Protection Agency. Having mastered the management of the national economy, the policy planners were to have moved on to quality-of-life issues. The "Great Society" was to become real.

What happened? Why does Camelot lie in ruin? Viet Nam and Watergate cannot explain everything forever. Intellectual error of monumental proportion has been made, and not exclusively by the ordinary politicians. Error also lies squarely with the economists.

The academic scribbler of the past who must bear substantial responsibility is Lord Keynes himself, whose ideas were uncritically accepted by American establishment economists. The mounting historical evidence of the effects of these ideas cannot continue to be ignored. Keynesian economics has turned the politicians loose; it has destroyed the effective constraint on politicians' ordinary appetites. Armed with the Keynesian message, politicians can spend and spend without the apparent necessity to tax. "Democracy in deficit" is descriptive, both of our economic plight and of the subject matter for this book.

The Political Economy

This book is an essay in political economy rather than in economic theory. Our focus is upon the political institutions through which economic policy must be implemented, policy which is, itself, ultimately derived from theory, good or bad. And central to our argument is the principle that the criteria for good theory are necessarily related to the political institutions of the society. The ideal normative theory of economic management for an authoritarian regime may fail completely for a regime that embodies participation by those who are to be managed. This necessary linkage or interdependence between the basic political structure of society and the economic theory of policy has never been properly recognized by economists, despite its elementary logic and its overwhelming empirical apparency.

Our critique of Keynesianism is concentrated on its political presuppositions, not on its internal theoretical structure. It is as if someone tried to make a jet engine operate by using the theory of the piston-driven machine. Nothing need be wrong with the theory save that it is wholly misapplied. This allows us largely but not completely to circumvent the troublesome and sometimes complex analyses in modern macroeconomic and monetary theory. This does not imply, however, that the applicable theory, that which is fully appropriate to the political institutions of a functioning democratic society, is simple and straightforward or, indeed, that this theory has been fully developed. Our discussion provides the setting within which such a theory might be pursued, and our plea is for economists to begin to think in terms of the political structure that we observe. But before this step can be taken, we must somehow reach agreement on the elements of the political decision process, on the model for policy making, to which any theory of policy is to be applied.

At this point, values cannot be left aside. If the Keynesian policy precepts for national economic management have failed, there are two ways of reacting. We may place the blame squarely on the vagaries of democratic politics, and propose that democratic decision making be replaced by more authoritarian rule. Or, alternatively, we can reject the applicability of the policy precepts in democratic structure, and try to invent and apply policy principles that are consistent with such structure. We choose the latter.[1] Our values dictate the democratic decision-making institutions should be maintained and that, to this end, inapplicable economic theories should be discarded as is necessary. If we observe democracy in deficit, we wish to repair the "deficit" part of this description, not to discard the "democracy" element.

A Review of the Record

We challenge the Keynesian theory of economic policy in this book. Our challenge will stand or fall upon the ability of our argument to persuade. There are two strings to our bow. We must first review both the pre-Keynesian

---

1. For a formulation of this choice alternative in a British context, see Robin Pringle, "Britain Hesitates before an Ineluctable Choice," *Banker* 125 (May 1975): 493–496.

and the post-Keynesian record. Forty years of history offers us a basis for at least preliminary assessment. We shall look carefully at the fiscal activities of the United States government before the Great Depression of the 1930s, before the publication of Keynes' *General Theory*.[2] The simple facts of budget balance or imbalance are important here, and these will not be neglected in the discussion of Chapter 2. More importantly for our purposes, however, we must try to determine the "principles" for budget making that informed the political decision makers. What precepts for "fiscal responsibility" were implicit in their behavior? How influential was the simple analogy between the individual and the government financial account? How did the balanced-budget norm act to constrain spending proclivities of politicians and parties?

There was no full-blown Keynesian "revolution" in the 1930s. The American acceptance of Keynesian ideas proceeded step by step from the Harvard economists, to economists in general, to the journalists, and, finally, to the politicians in power. This gradual spread of Keynesian notions, as well as the accompanying demise of the old-fashioned principles for financial responsibility, is documented in Chapters 3 and 4. The Keynesian brigades first had to storm the halls of ivy, for only then would they have a base from which to capture the minds of the public and the halls of Congress. Chapter 3 documents the triumph of Keynesianism throughout the groves of academe, while Chapter 4 describes the infusion of Keynesianism into the general consciousness of the body politic—its emergence as an element of our general cultural climate.

Even if our review of the historical record is convincing, no case is established for raising the alarm. What is of such great moment if elected politicians do respond to the Keynesian messages in somewhat biased manner? What is there about budget deficits to arouse concern? How can the burden of debt be passed along to our grandchildren? Is inflation the monster that it is sometimes claimed to be? Why not learn to live with it, especially if unemployment can be kept within bounds? If Keynesian economics has and can secure high-level employment, why not give it the highest marks, even when recognizing its by-product generation of inflation and relatively expanding government? These are the questions that require serious analysis

2. John Maynard Keynes, *The General Theory of Employment, Interest, and Money* (New York: Harcourt, Brace, 1936).

and discussion, because these are the questions that most economists would ask of us; they are explored in Chapter 5.

The Theory of Public Choice

Our second instrument of persuasion is a theory for decision making in democracy, a theory of public choice, which was so long neglected by economists. This is developed in Chapters 6 through 9. Keynes was not a democrat, but, rather, looked upon himself as a potential member of an enlightened ruling elite. Political institutions were largely irrelevant for the formulation of his policy presumptions. The application of the Keynesian precepts within a working political democracy, however, would often require politicians to undertake actions that would reduce their prospects for survival. Should we then be surprised that the Keynesian democratic political institutions will produce policy responses contrary to those that would be forthcoming from some idealized application of the norms in the absence of political feedback?

In Chapter 7, it is shown that ordinary political representatives in positions of either legislative or executive authority will behave quite differently when confronted with taxing and spending alternatives than would their benevolently despotic counterparts, those whom Keynes viewed as making policy, whose behavior is examined in Chapter 6. In Chapter 8, the analysis of Chapter 7 is extended to the behavior of monetary authorities, and monetary decisions are considered as endogenous rather than as exogenous variables.

A crucial feature of our argument is the ability of political and fiscal institutions to influence the outcomes of political processes, a subject that we explore in Chapter 9. Institutions matter in our analysis. While this position is generally accepted by those who call themselves "Keynesians," it is disputed by many of those who consider themselves "anti-" or "non-Keynesians." These latter analysts argue that institutions are generally irrelevant. With respect to institutions, we are like the Keynesians, for we do not let an infatuation with abstract models destroy our sense of reality. Instead, we accept the proposition that institutions, like ideas, have consequences that are not at all obvious at the time of their inception, a point that Richard Weaver noted so memorably.[3] At the same time, however, our view of the nature of a free-enterprise

3. See Richard M. Weaver, *Ideas Have Consequences* (Chicago: University of Chicago Press, 1948).

economic order is distinctly non-Keynesian, although "Keynesianism" must to some extent be distinguished from the "economics of Keynes."[4]

The theory of public choice discussed in Chapters 6–9 is not at all complex, and it offers satisfactory explanations of the post-Keynesian fiscal record. The Keynesian defense must be, however, that the theory is indeed too simplistic, that politicians can and will behave differently from the predictions of the theory. We do not, of course, rule out the ability of politicians, intelligent persons all, to learn the Keynesian lessons. But will the voters-citizens, who determine who their political representatives will be, accept the proffered wisdom? This is a tougher question, and the familiar call for more economic education of the public has long since become a tiresome relic. The Keynesian who relies on a more sophisticated electorate to reverse the accumulating record leans on a frail reed.

Fiscal and Monetary Reform

In the last three chapters of the book, we return to what may be considered the main theme. Even the ardent Keynesians recognized, quite early, that some replacement for the fiscal rule of balanced budgets might be required as guidance for even the enlightened politicians. In Chapter 10, we examine the alternative rules for fiscal responsibility that have been advanced and used in the discussion of fiscal and budgetary policy. These include the rule for budget balance over the business cycle, and, more importantly, the rule for budget balance at full employment which continues to inform the official economic pronouncements from Washington, even if it is largely disregarded in practice.

Chapter 11 represents our response to what will seem to many to be our most vulnerable point. What about unemployment? Our criticism of the implications of the Keynesian teachings may be widely accepted, up to a point. But how are we to respond to the argument that the maintenance of high-level employment is the overriding objective for national economic policy,

4. See Axel Leijonhufvud, *On Keynesian Economics and the Economics of Keynes* (London: Oxford University Press, 1968); and G. L. S. Shackle, "Keynes and Today's Establishment in Economic Theory: A View," *Journal of Economic Literature* 11 (June 1973): 516–519. A somewhat different perspective is presented in Leland B. Yeager, "The Keynesian Diversion," *Western Economic Journal* 11 (June 1973): 150–163.

and that only the Keynesian teachings offer resolution? These questions inform this chapter, in which we question the foundations of such prevalent attitudes.

Chapter 12 offers our own substantive proposals for fiscal and monetary reform. Our emphasis here is on the necessity that the reforms introduced be treated as genuine constitutional measures, rules that are designed to constrain the short-run expedient behavior of politicians. Our emphasis here is in the long-range nature of reform, rather than on the details of particular proposals. To avoid charges of incompleteness and omission, however, we advance explicit suggestions for constitutional change, and notably for the adoption of a constitutional amendment requiring budget balance.

2. The Old-Time Fiscal Religion

Classical Fiscal Principle

The history of both fiscal principle and fiscal practice may reasonably be divided into pre- and post-Keynesian periods. The Keynesian breakpoint is stressed concisely by Hugh Dalton, the textbook writer whose own political career was notoriously brief. In the post-Keynesian editions of his *Principles of Public Finance,* Dalton said:

> The new approach to budgetary policy owes more to Keynes than to any other man. Thus it is just that we should speak of "the Keynesian revolution." . . . We may now free ourselves from the old and narrow conception of balancing the budget, no matter over what period, and move towards the new and wider conception of balancing the whole economy.[1]

In this chapter, we shall examine briefly the pre-Keynesian history, in terms of both the articulation of fiscal principle and the implementation of fiscal practice. As noted at the beginning of Chapter 1, the pre-Keynesian or "classical" principles can perhaps best be summarized in the analogy between the state and the family. Prudent financial conduct by the government was conceived in basically the same image as that by the family or the firm. Frugality, not profligacy, was accepted as the cardinal virtue, and this norm assumed practical shape in the widely shared principle that public budgets should be in balance, if not in surplus, and that deficits were to be tolerated only in extraordinary circumstances. Substantial and continuing deficits were interpreted as the mark of fiscal folly. Principles of sound business practice were

---

1. Hugh Dalton, *Principles of Public Finance,* 4th ed. (London: Routledge and Kegan Paul, 1954), p. 221.

also held relevant to the fiscal affairs of government. When capital expenditures were financed by debt, sinking funds for amortization were to be established and maintained. The substantial attention paid to the use and operation of sinking funds in the fiscal literature during the whole pre-Keynesian era attests to the strength with which these basic classical principles were held.[2]

Textbooks and treatises embodied the noncontroverted principle that public budgets should be in balance. C. F. Bastable, one of the leading public-finance scholars of the late nineteenth and early twentieth centuries, in commenting on "The Relation of Expenditure and Receipts," suggested that

> under normal conditions, there ought to be a balance between these two sides [expenditure and revenue] of financial activity. Outlay should not exceed income, ... tax revenue ought to be kept up to the amount required to defray expenses.[3]

Bastable recognized the possibility of extenuating circumstances, which led him to modify his statement of the principle of budget balance by stating:

> This general principle must, however, admit of modifications. Temporary deficits and surpluses cannot be avoided. . . . All that can be claimed is a substantial approach to a balance in the two sides of the account. The safest rule for practice is that which lays down the expediency of *estimating for a moderate surplus,* by which the possibility of a deficit will be reduced to a minimum. [Italics supplied][4]

Classical or pre-Keynesian fiscal principles, in other words, supported a budget surplus during normal times so as to provide a cushion for more troublesome periods. And similar statements can be found throughout the pre-Keynesian fiscal literature.[5]

Aside from the simple, and basically intuitive, analogy drawn between gov-

2. For a thorough examination of these classical principles and how they functioned as an unwritten constitutional constraint during the pre-Keynesian era, see William Breit, "Starving the Leviathan: Balanced Budget Prescriptions before Keynes" (Paper presented at the Conference on Federal Fiscal Responsibility, March 1976), to be published in a conference volume.

3. C. F. Bastable, *Public Finance,* 3rd ed. (London: Macmillan, 1903), p. 611.

4. Ibid.

5. For a survey of the balanced-budget principle, see Jesse Burkhead, "The Balanced Budget," *Quarterly Journal of Economics* 68 (May 1954): 191–216.

ernments and individuals and business firms, these rules for "sound finance" were reinforced by two distinct analytical principles, only one of which was made explicit in the economic policy analysis of the period. The dominant principle (one that was expressed clearly by Adam Smith and incorporated into the theory of economic policy) was that resort to debt finance by government provided evidence of public profligacy, and, furthermore, a form of profligacy that imposed fiscal burdens on subsequent taxpayers. Put starkly, debt finance enabled people living currently to enrich themselves at the expense of people living in the future. These notions about debt finance, which were undermined by the Keynesian revolution, reinforced adherence to a balanced-budget principle of fiscal conduct. We shall describe these principles of debt finance and debt burden more carefully in a subsequent section of this chapter.

A second analytical principle emerged more than a century after Smith's *Wealth of Nations,* and it was not explicitly incorporated into the norms for policy. But it may have been implicitly recognized. It is important because it reinforces the classical principles from a different and essentially political or public-choice perspective. In 1896, Knut Wicksell noted that an individual could make an informed, rational assessment of various proposals for public expenditure only if he were confronted with a tax bill at the same time.[6] Moreover, to facilitate such comparison, Wicksell suggested that the total costs of any proposed expenditure program should be apportioned among the individual members of the political community. These were among the institutional features that he thought necessary to make reasonably efficient fiscal decisions in a democracy. Effective democratic government requires institutional arrangements that force citizens to take account of the costs of government as well as the benefits, and to do so simultaneously. The Wicksellian emphasis was on making political decisions more efficient, on ensuring that costs be properly weighed against benefits. A norm of balancing the fiscal decision or choice process, if not a formal balancing of the budget, emerges directly from the Wicksellian analysis.

6. Knut Wicksell, *Finanztheoretische Untersuchungen* (Jena: Gustav Fischer, 1896). Translated as "A New Principle of Just Taxation" in R. A. Musgrave and A. T. Peacock, eds., *Classics in the Theory of Public Finance* (London: Macmillan, 1958), pp. 72–118.

Fiscal Practice in Pre-Keynesian Times

Pre-Keynesian fiscal practice was clearly informed by the classical notions of fiscal responsibility, as an examination of the record will show.[7] This fiscal history was not one of a rigidly balanced budget defined on an annual accounting basis. There were considerable year-to-year fluctuations in receipts, in expenditures, and in the resulting surplus or deficit. Nonetheless, a pattern is clearly discernible: Deficits emerged primarily during periods of war; budgets normally produced surpluses during peacetime, and these surpluses were used to retire the debt created during war emergencies.[8]

The years immediately following the establishment of the American Republic in 1789 were turbulent. There was war with the Indians in the Northwest; the Whiskey Rebellion erupted; and relations with England were deteriorating and fears of war were strong. Federal government budgets were generally in deficit during this period, and by 1795 the gross national debt was $83.8 million. But by 1811 this total had been reduced nearly by half, to $45.2 million. And during the sixteen years of this 1795–1811 period, there were fourteen years of surplus and two years of a deficit. Moreover, the surpluses tended to be relatively large, averaging in the vicinity of $2.5 million in federal budgets with total expenditures that averaged around $8 million.

The War of 1812 brought forth a new sequence of budget deficits that lasted through 1815. The cumulative deficit over this four-year period slightly exceeded $65 million, which was more than one-half of the cumulative public expenditure during this same period. Once again, however, the gross national debt of $127 million at the end of 1815 was steadily reduced during the subsequent two decades. In the twenty-one years from 1816 through 1836, there were eighteen years of surplus, and the gross debt had fallen to $337,000 by the end of 1836.

John W. Kearny, writing in 1887 on the fiscal history of the 1789–1835 period, reflected the sentiment that the retirement of public debt was an im-

---

7. Numerical details by year can be found in the "Statistical Appendix" to the *Annual Report of the Secretary of the Treasury on the State of the Finances* (Washington: U.S. Government Printing Office, 1976).

8. For a survey of our budgetary history through 1958, see Lewis H. Kimmel, *Federal Budget and Fiscal Policy, 1789–1958* (Washington: Brookings Institution, 1959).

portant political issue at that time. The primary vehicle for accomplishing this policy of debt retirement was the Sinking-Fund Act of 1795, as amended in 1802. Under these acts, substantial revenues were earmarked and set aside for debt retirement. Kearny's assessment of the 1795 act expresses clearly the attitude toward deficit finance and public debt that prevailed:

> The Act of the 3d of March, 1795, is an event of importance in the financial history of the country. It was the consummation of what remained unfinished in our system of public credit, in that it publicly recognized, and ingrafted on that system, three essential principles, the regular operation of which can alone *prevent a progressive accumulation of debt:* first of all it established distinctive revenues for the payment of the interest of the public debt as well as for the reimbursement of the principal within a determinate period; secondly, it directed imperatively their application to the debt alone; and thirdly it pledged the faith of the Government that the appointed revenues should continue to be levied and collected and appropriated to these objects until the whole debt should be redeemed. [Italics supplied][9]

The depression that followed the Panic of 1837 lasted throughout the administration of Martin Van Buren and halfway through the administration of William Henry Harrison and John Tyler, terminating only in 1843. This depression seems clearly to have been the most severe of the nineteenth century and has been described as "one of the longest periods of sustained contraction in the nation's history, rivaled only by the downswing of 1929–33."[10] During this seven-year period of economic stress, there were six years of deficit, and the national debt had soared to $32.7 million by the end of 1843.

Once again, as stability returned, the normal pattern of affairs was resumed. Three consecutive surpluses were run, reducing the national debt to $15.6 million by the end of 1846. With the advent of the Mexican-American War, deficits emerged again during 1847–1849, and the gross debt climbed to $63.5 million by the end of 1849. Eight years of surplus then ensued, followed

---

9. John W. Kearny, *Sketch of American Finances, 1789–1835* (1887; reprint ed., New York: Greenwood Press, 1968), pp. 43–44.

10. Lance E. Davis, Jonathan R. T. Hughes, and Duncan M. McDougall, *American Economic History*, rev. ed. (Homewood, Ill.: Richard D. Irwin, 1965), p. 420. See also Reginald C. McGrane, *The Panic of 1837* (New York: Russell and Russell, 1965).

by two years of deficit, and then the Civil War. By the end of 1865, the gross public debt of the United States government had increased dramatically to $2.7 billion.

Once hostilities ceased, however, twenty-eight consecutive years of budget surplus resulted. By the end of 1893, the gross debt had been reduced by two-thirds, to $961 million. The rate of reduction of outstanding debt was substantial, with approximately one-quarter of public expenditure during this period being devoted to debt amortization. Deficits emerged in 1894 and 1895, and, later in the decade, the Spanish-American War brought forth four additional years of deficit. By the end of 1899, the gross national debt stood at $1.4 billion.

The years prior to World War I were a mixture of surplus and deficit, with a slight tendency toward surplus serving to reduce the debt to $1.2 billion by the end of 1916. World War I brought three years of deficit, and the national debt stood at $25.5 billion by the end of 1918. There then followed eleven consecutive years of surplus, which reduced the national debt to $16.2 billion by 1930. The Great Depression and World War II then combined to produce sixteen consecutive years of deficit, after which the gross national debt stood at $169.4 billion in 1946.

Until 1946, then, the story of our fiscal practice was largely a consistent one, with budget surpluses being the normal rule, and with deficits emerging primarily during periods of war and severe depression. The history of fiscal practice coincided with a theory of debt finance that held that resort to debt issue provided a means of reducing present burdens in exchange for the obligation to take on greater burdens in the future. It was only during some such extraordinary event as a war or a major depression that debt finance seemed to be justified.

While the history of our fiscal practice did not change through 1946, fiscal theory began to change during the 1930s. One of the elements of this change was the emerging dominance of a theory of the burden of public debt that had been widely discredited. The classical theory of public debt, which we shall describe more fully in the next section, suggests that debt issue is a means by which present taxpayers can shift part of the cost of government on the shoulders of taxpayers in future periods. The competing theory of public debt, which had been variously suggested by earlier writers, was embraced anew by Keynesian economists, so much so that it quickly became the orthodox one, and well may be called the "Keynesian" theory of public debt. This theory explicitly denies that debt finance places any burden on future tax-payers. It suggests instead that citizens who live during the period when public expenditures are made always and necessarily bear the cost of public services, regardless of whether those services are financed through taxation or through debt creation. This shift in ideas on public debt was, in turn, vital in securing acquiescence to deficit financing. There was no longer any reason for opposing deficit financing on basically moral grounds. This Keynesian theory of debt burden, however, is a topic to be covered in the next chapter; the task at hand is to examine briefly the Smithian or classical theory.

Balanced Budgets, Debt Burdens, and Fiscal Responsibility

Pre-Keynesian debt theory held that there is one fundamental difference between tax finance and debt finance that is obscured by the Keynesians. In the pre-Keynesian view, a choice between tax finance and debt finance is a choice of the timing of the payments for public expenditure. Tax finance places the burden of payment squarely upon those members of the political community during the period when the expenditure decision is made. Debt finance, on the other hand, postpones payment until interest and amortization payments on debt come due. Debt finance enables those people living at the time of fiscal decision to shift payment onto those living in later periods, which may, of course, be the same group, especially if the period over which the debt is amortized is short.

In earlier works, we have offered an analytical defense of the classical theory of public debt, and especially as it is compared with its putative Keynesian replacement.[11] We shall not, at this point, repeat details of other works. Nonetheless, a summary analysis of the basic classical theory will be helpful, since the broad acceptance of this theory by the public and by the politicians was surely a significant element in cementing and reinforcing the private-public finance analogy.

---

11. See James M. Buchanan, *Public Principles of Public Debt* (Homewood, Ill.: Richard D. Irwin, 1958); and James M. Buchanan and Richard E. Wagner, *Public Debt in a Democratic Society* (Washington: American Enterprise Institute, 1967).

What happens when a government borrows? Before this question may be answered, we must specify both the fiscal setting that is assumed to be present and the alternative courses of action that might be followed. The purpose of borrowing is, presumably, to finance public spending. It seems, therefore, appropriate to assume that a provisional decision has been made to spend public funds. Having made this decision, the question reduces to one of choice among alternative means of financing. There are only three possibilities: (1) taxation, (2) public borrowing or debt issue, and (3) money creation. We shall, at this point, leave money creation out of account, because the Keynesian attack was launched on the classical theory of public borrowing, not upon the traditionally accepted theory of the effects of money creation. The theory of public debt reduces to a comparison between the effects of taxation and public debt issue, on the assumption that the public spending is fixed. The question becomes: When a government borrows, what happens that does not happen when it finances the same outlay through current taxation?

With borrowing, the command over real resources, over purchasing power, is surrendered voluntarily to government by those who purchase the bonds sold by the government, in a private set of choices independent of the political process. This is simply an ordinary exchange. Those who purchase these claims are not purchasing or paying for the benefits that are promised by the government outlays. They are simply paying for the obligations on the part of the government to provide them with an interest return in future periods and to amortize the principal on some determinate schedule. (This extremely simple point, the heart of the whole classical theory of public debt, is the source of major intellectual confusion.) These bond purchasers are the *only* persons in the community who give up or sacrifice commands over current resource use, who give up private investment or consumption prospects, in order that the government may obtain command over the resources which the budgetary outlays indicate to be desirable.

But if this sacrifice of purchasing power is made through a set of voluntary exchanges for bonds, who is really "purchasing," and by implication "paying for," the benefits that the budgetary outlays promise to provide? The ultimate "purchasers" of such benefits, under the public debt as under the taxation alternative, are all the members of the political community, at least as these are represented through the standard political decision-making process. A decision to "purchase" these benefits is presumably made via the political rules and institutions in being. But who "pays for" these benefits? Who suffers private costs which may then be balanced off against the private benefits offered by the publicly supplied services? Under taxation, these costs are imposed directly on the citizens, as determined by the existing rules for tax or cost sharing. Under public borrowing, by contrast, these costs are not imposed currently, during the budgetary period when the outlays are made. Instead, these costs are *postponed* or put off until later periods when interest and amortization payments come due. This elementary proposition applies to public borrowing in precisely the same way that it applies to private borrowing; the classical analogy between private and public finance seems to hold without qualification.

Indeed, the whole purpose of borrowing, private or public, should be to facilitate an expansion of outlay by putting off the necessity for meeting the costs. The basic institution of debt is designed to modify the time sequence between outlay and payment. As such, and again for both the private and the public borrower, there is no general normative rule against borrowing as opposed to current financing, and especially with respect to capital outlays. There is nothing in the classical theory of public debt that allows us to condemn government borrowing at all times and places.

Both for the family or firm and for the government, there exist norms for financial responsibility, for prudent fiscal conduct. Resort to borrowing, to debt issue, should be limited to those situations in which spending needs are "bunched" in time, owing either to such extraordinary circumstances as natural emergencies or disasters or to the lumpy requirements of a capital investment program. In either case, borrowing should be accompanied by a scheduled program of amortization. When debt is incurred because of the investment of funds in capital creation, amortization should be scheduled to coincide with the useful or productive life of the capital assets. Guided by this principle of fiscal responsibility, a government may, for example, incur public debts to construct a road or highway network, provided that these debts are scheduled for amortization over the years during which the network is anticipated to yield benefits or returns to the citizens of the political community. Such considerations as these provide the source for separating current and capital budgets in the accounts of governments, with the implication that principles of financing may differ as the type of outlay differs. These norms incorporate the notion that only the prospect of benefits in periods subsequent to the outlay makes legitimate the postponing or putting off of the costs of this outlay. There is nothing in this classically familiar argument, however, that suggests that the costs will somehow disappear because the benefits accrue in later periods, an absurd distortion that some of the more extreme Keynesian arguments would seem to introduce.

The classical rules for responsible borrowing, public or private, are clear enough, but the public-finance–private-finance analogy may break down when the effects of irresponsible or imprudent financial conduct are analyzed. The dangers of irresponsible borrowing seem greater for governments than for private families or firms. For this reason, more stringent constraints may need to be placed on public than on private debt issue. The difference lies in the specification and identification of the liability or obligation incurred under debt financing in the two cases. If an individual borrows, he incurs a personal liability. The creditor holds a claim against the assets of the person who initially makes the decision to borrow, and the borrower cannot readily shift his liability to others. There are few willing recipients of liabilities. If the borrower dies, the creditor has a claim against his estate.

Compare this with the situation of an individual who is a citizen in a political community whose governmental units borrow to finance current outlay. At the time of the borrowing decision, the individual citizen is not assigned a specific and determinate share of the fiscal liability that the public debt represents. He may, of course, sense that some such liability exists for the whole community, but there is no identifiable claim created against his privately owned assets. The obligations are those of the political community, generally considered, rather than those of identified members of the community. If, then, a person can succeed in escaping what might be considered his "fair" share of the liability by some change in the tax-share structure, or by some shift in the membership of the community through migration, or merely by growth in the domestic population, he will not behave as if the public debt is equivalent to private debt.

Because of this difference in the specification and identification of liability in private and public debt, we should predict that persons will be somewhat less prudent in issuing the latter than the former. That is to say, the pressures brought to bear on governmental decision makers to constrain irresponsible borrowing may not be comparable to those that the analogous private borrower would incorporate within his own behavioral calculus. The relative absence of such public or voter constraints might lead elected politicians, those who explicitly make spending, taxing, and borrowing decisions for governments, to borrow even when the conditions for responsible debt issues are not present. It is in recognition of such proclivities that classical principles of public fiscal responsibility incorporate explicit limits on resort to borrowing as a financing alternative, and which also dictate that sinking funds or other comparable provisions be made for amortization of loans at the time of any initial spending-borrowing commitment.[12]

Without some such constraints, the classical theory embodies the prediction of a political scenario with cumulatively increasing public debt, unaccompanied by comparable values in accumulating public assets, a debt which, quite literally, places a mortgage claim against the future income of the productive members of the political community. As new generations of voters-taxpayers appear, they would, under this scenario, face fiscal burdens that owe their origins exclusively to the profligacy of their forebears. To the extent that citizens, and the politicians who act for them in making fiscal choices, regard members of future generations as lineal extensions of their own lives, the implicit fears of overextended public credit might never be realized. But for the reasons noted above, classical precepts suggest that dependence could not be placed on such potential concern for taxpayers in future periods. The effective time horizon, both for members of the voting public and for the elected politicians alike, seems likely to be short, an implicit presumption of the whole classical construction.

This is not, of course, to deny that the effects on taxpayers in later budgetary periods do not serve, and cannot serve, as constraints on public borrowing. So long as decision makers act on the knowledge that debt issue does, in fact, shift the cost of outlay forward in time, some limit is placed on irresponsible behavior. That is to say, even in the absence of classically inspired institutional constraints on public debt, a generalized public acceptance of the classical theory of public debt would, in itself, exert an important inhibiting effect. It is in this context that the putative replacement of the classical

---

12. For an analysis of the possibilities for debt abuse within a political democracy, see James M. Buchanan, *Public Finance in Democratic Process* (Chapel Hill: University of North Carolina Press, 1967), pp. 256–266; and Richard E. Wagner, "Optimality in Local Debt Limitation," *National Tax Journal* 23 (September 1970): 297–305.

theory by the Keynesian theory can best be evaluated. The latter denies that debt finance implements an intertemporal shift of realized burden or cost of outlay, quite apart from the question as to the possible desirability or undesirability of this method of financing. The existence of opportunities for cumulative political profligacy is viewed as impossible; there are no necessarily adverse consequences for future taxpayers. The selling of the Keynesian theory of debt burden, which we shall examine in the next chapter, was a necessary first step in bringing about a democracy in deficit.

Fiscal Principles and Keynesian Economic Theory

There was a genuine "Keynesian revolution" in fiscal principles, the effects of which we attempt to chronicle in this book. But we should not overlook the fact that this fiscal revolution was embedded within the more comprehensive Keynesian theory of economic process. As Chapters 3 and 4 will discuss in some detail, there was a shift in the vision or paradigm for the operation of the whole economy. Without this, there would have been no need for the revolutionary shift in attitudes about fiscal precepts.

This is illustrated in the competing theories of public debt, noted above. Analyses of the effects of public debt closely similar to those associated with those advanced under Keynesian banners had been advanced long before the 1930s and in various countries and by various writers.[13] These attacks on the classical theory were never fully effective in capturing the minds of economists, because they were not accompanied by a shift away from the underlying paradigm of neoclassical economics. A nonclassical theory of public debt superimposed on an essentially classical theory of economic process could, at best, have been relevant for government budget making. But the nonclassical theory of public debt advanced by the Keynesians was superimposed on the nonclassical theory of economic process, a theory which, in its normative application, elevated deficit financing to a central role. A change in the effective fiscal constitution implied not only a release of politicians from the constraining influences that prevented approval of larger debt-financed public budgets, but also a means for securing the more important macroeconomic

13. For a summary of the literature, see Buchanan, *Public Principles of Public Debt*, pp. 16−20.

objectives of increased real income and employment.[14] To be sure, it was recognized that deficit financing might also increase governmental outlays, possibly an objective in itself, but the strictly Keynesian emphasis was on the effects on the economy rather than on the probable size of the budget as such. And it was this instrumental value of budget deficits, and by implication of public debt, that led economists to endorse, often enthusiastically and without careful analysis, theoretical constructions that would have been held untenable if examined independently and on their own.

There is, of course, no necessary relationship between the theory of public debt and the theory of economic process. A sophisticated analysis can incorporate a strictly classical theory of public debt into a predominantly Keynesian theory of income and employment. Or, conversely, a modern non-Keynesian monetarist could possibly accept the no-transfer or Keynesian theory of debt burden. The same could scarcely be said for fiscal principles, considered in total. The old-time fiscal religion, that which incorporates both the classical theory of debt and the precept which calls for budget balance, could not readily be complementary to an analysis of the economic process and policy that is fully Keynesian. In terms of intellectual history, it was the acceptance of Keynesian economic theory which produced the revolution in ideas about fiscal principles and practice, rather than the reverse.

---

14. For examinations of this categorical shift in the scope of fiscal policy during the 1930s, see Ursula K. Hicks, *British Public Finances: Their Structure and Development, 1880–1952* (London: Oxford University Press, 1954); and Lawrence C. Pierce, *The Politics of Fiscal Policy Formation* (Pacific Palisades, Calif.: Goodyear, 1971). With reference to Great Britain, Hicks noted:

> Fiscal policy in the sense of a purposeful marshalling of the armoury of public finance in order to influence the level of incomes cannot be said to have been recognized as an art before the middle or late 1930s. Up to that time considerations of public finance ran in terms only of the effects of individual taxes and outlays, on particular aspects of economic life, without regard to the total effect. [p. 140]

With reference to the United States, Pierce observed:

> Until the late 1930s, the role of the government budget was limited to providing public services, raising taxes to pay for them, and, less often, influencing the distribution of income among regions and individuals. It is only since the late 1930s that economists and political leaders have come to believe that they can also use the federal budget to help avoid most of the economic ills associated with high levels of unemployment, price inflation, and economic stagnation. [p. 1]

The Fiscal Constitution

Whether they are incorporated formally in some legally binding and explicitly constitutional document or merely in a set of customary, traditional, and widely accepted precepts, we can describe the prevailing rules guiding fiscal choice as a "fiscal constitution." As we have noted, thoughout the pre-Keynesian era, the effective fiscal constitution was based on the central principle that public finance and private finance are analogous, and that the norms for prudent conduct are similar. Barring extraordinary circumstances, public expenditures were supposed to be financed by taxation, just as private spending was supposed to be financed from income.

The pre-Keynesian or classical fiscal constitution was not written in any formal set of rules. It was, nonetheless, almost universally accepted.[15] And its importance lay in its influence in constraining the profligacy of all persons, members of the public along with the politicians who acted for them. Because expenditures were expected to be financed from taxation, there was less temptation for dominant political coalitions to use the political process to implement direct income transfers among groups. Once the expenditure-taxation nexus was broken, however, the opportunities for such income transfers were increased. Harry G. Johnson, for instance, has advanced the thesis that the modern tendency toward ever-increasing budget deficits results from such redistributional games. Governments increasingly enact public expenditure programs that confer benefits on special segments of the population, with the cost borne by taxpayers generally. Many such programs might not be financed in the face of strenuous taxpayer resistance, but might well secure acceptance under debt finance. The hostility to the expenditure programs is reduced in this way, and budgets rise; intergroup income transfers multiply.[16]

Few could quarrel with the simple thesis that the effective fiscal constitution in the United States was transformed by Keynesian economics. The old-time fiscal religion is no more. But, one might reasonably ask, "so what?" The destruction of the classical principles of fiscal policy was to have made

15. See Breit.
16. Harry G. Johnson, "Living with Inflation," *Banker* 125 (August 1975): 863–864.

possible major gains in overall economic performance. If so, we should not mourn the passing of such outmoded principles.

Keynesianism offered the promise of replacing the old with a better, more efficient fiscal constitution. By using government to control aggregate macroeconomic variables, cyclical fluctuations in economic activity were to be damped; the economy was to have both less unemployment and less inflation. If interpreted as prediction, the Keynesian promise has not been kept. The economy of the 1970s has not performed satisfactorily, despite the Keynesian-inspired direction of policy.

3. First, the Academic Scribblers

John Maynard Keynes was a speculator, in ideas as well as in foreign currencies, and his speculation was scarcely idle. He held an arrogant confidence in the ideas that he adopted, at least while he held them, along with a disdain for the virtues of temporal consistency. His objective, with *The General Theory of Employment, Interest, and Money* (1936), was to secure a permanent shift in the policies of governments, and he recognized that the conversion of the academic scribblers, in this case the economists, was a necessary first step. "It is my fellow economists, not the general public, whom I must convince."[1] In the economic disorder of the Great Depression, there were many persons—politicians, scholars, publicists—in America and elsewhere, who advanced policy proposals akin to those that were to be called "Keynesian." But it was Keynes, and Keynes alone, who captured the minds of the economists (or most of them) by changing their vision of the economic process.

Without Keynes, government budgets would have become unbalanced, as they did before Keynes, during periods of depression and war. Without Keynes, governments would have varied the rate of money creation over time and place, with bad and good consequences. Without Keynes, World War II would have happened, and the economies of Western democracies would have been pulled out of the lingering stagnation of the 1930s. Without Keynes, substantially full employment and an accompanying inflationary threat would have described the postwar years. But these events of history would have been conceived and described differently, then and now, without the towering Keynesian presence. Without Keynes, the proclivities of ordinary politicians would have been held in check more adequately in the 1960s

---

1. John Maynard Keynes, *The General Theory of Employment, Interest, and Money* (New York: Harcourt, Brace, 1936), p. vi.

and 1970s. Without Keynes, modern budgets would not be quite so bloated, with the threat of more to come, and inflation would not be the clear and present danger to the free society that it has surely now become. The legacy or heritage of Lord Keynes is the putative intellectual legitimacy provided to the natural and predictable political biases toward deficit spending, inflation, and the growth of government.

Our objective in this chapter is to examine the Keynesian impact on the ideas of economists, on the "Keynesian revolution" in economic theory and policy as discussed within the ivied walls of academia. By necessity as well as intent, our treatment will be general and without detail, since our purpose is not that of offering a contribution to intellectual or scientific history, but, rather, that of providing an essential element in any understanding of the ultimate political consequences of Keynesian ideas.[2]

"Classical Economics," a Construction in Straw?

Keynes set out to change the way that economists looked at the national economy. A first step was the construction of a convenient and vulnerable target, which emerged as the "classical economists," who were only partially identified but who were, in fact, somewhat provincially located in England. With scarcely a sidewise glance at the institutional prerequisites, Keynes aimed directly at the jugular of the targeted model, the self-equilibrating mechanism of the market economy. In the Keynesian description, the classical economist remained steadfast in his vision of a stable economy that contained within it self-adjusting reactions to exogenous shocks, reactions that would ensure that the economy as a whole, as well as in its particular sectors, would return toward a determinate set of equilibrium values. Furthermore, these values were determinate at plausibly desired levels. Following Ricardo and rejecting Mal-

2. In various works, Professor Axel Leijonhufvud of UCLA has examined the impact of Keynesian ideas on economists in some detail. We are indebted to his insights here, which supplement our much less comprehensive examination of the intellectual history.

Robert Skidelsky, "Keynes and the Revolt against the Victorians," *Spectator*, 1 May 1976, pp. 14–16, contrasts the Keynesian and the Victorian world views. While the Victorian emphasis was on a goal-directed life, the Keynesian emphasis stressed living in the present. Keynes' assault on saving and thrift is one consequence of this shift in Weltanschauung.

thus, the classical economists denied the prospects of a general glut on markets.[3]

It is not within our purpose here to discuss the methodological or the analytical validity of the Keynesian argument against its allegedly classical opposition. We shall not attempt to discuss our own interpretation of just what pre-Keynesian economics actually was. The attack was launched, not upon that which might have existed, but upon an explicitly defined variant, which may or may not have been caricature. And the facts of intellectual history attest to the success of the venture. Economists of the twentieth century's middle decades conceived "classical economics" in the image conjured for them by Keynes, and they interpret the "revolution" as the shift away from that image. This is all that need concern us here.

In this image, "classical economics" embodied the presumption that there existed built-in equilibrating forces which ensured that a capitalistic economy would generate continuing prosperity and high-level employment. Exogenous shocks might, of course, occur, but these would trigger reactions that would quickly, and surely, tend to restore overall equilibrium at high-employment levels. Such an image seemed counter to the observed facts of the 1920s in Britain and of the 1930s almost everywhere. National economies seemed to be floundering, not prospering, and unemployment seemed to be both pervasive and permanent.

Keynes boldly challenged the basic classical paradigm of his construction. He denied the very existence of the self-equilibrating forces of the capitalist economy. He rejected the extension of the Marshallian conception of particular market equilibrium to the economy as a whole, and to the aggregates that might be introduced to describe it. A national economy might attain "equilibrium," but there need be no assurance that the automatic forces of the market would produce acceptably high and growing real output and high-level employment.[4]

Again we need not and shall not trace out the essential Keynesian argument, in any of its many variants, and there would be little that we might add

3. For a recent, careful restatement of this position, see W. H. Hutt, *A Rehabilitation of Say's Law* (Athens: Ohio University Press, 1974).

4. See Axel Leijonhufvud, "Effective Demand Failures," *Swedish Journal of Economics* 75 (March 1973): 27–48, for a description of these two alternative paradigms and a discussion of how they influence the economist's analytical perspective.

to the still-burgeoning literature of critical reinterpretation and analysis. What is important for us is the observed intellectual success of the central Keynesian challenge. From the early 1940s, most professionally trained economists looked at "the economy" differently from the way they might have looked at the selfsame phenomenon in the early 1920s or early 1930s. In a general sense of the phrase, a paradigm shift took place.

Before Keynes, economists of almost all persuasions implicitly measured the social productivity of their own efforts by the potential gains in allocative efficiency which might be forthcoming upon the rational incorporation of economists' continuing institutional criticisms of political reality. How much increase in social value might be generated by a shift of resources from *this* to *that* use? Keynes sought to change, and succeeded in changing, this role for economists. Allocative efficiency, as a meaningful and desirable social objective, was not rejected. Instead, it was simply relegated to a second level of importance by comparison with the "pure efficiency" that was promised by an increase in the sheer volume of employment itself. It is little wonder that economists became excited about their greatly enhanced role and that they came to see themselves as new persons of standing.

Once converted, economists could have readily been predicted to allow Keynes the role of pied piper. But how were they to be converted? They had to be convinced that the economic disaster of the Great Depression was something more than the consequence of specific mistakes in monetary policy, and that correction required more than temporary measures. Keynes accomplished this aspect of the conversion by presenting a *general* theory of the aggregative economic process, one that appeared to explain the events of the 1930s as one possible natural outcome of market interaction rather than as an aberrant result produced by policy lapses.[5] In this general theory, there is

---

5. One important element in the articulation of this Keynesian position was the presence of persistently high unemployment throughout the 1930s. Such a record seemed to vitiate the classical belief in a self-adjusting economy. This entire record, it now turns out, is false, for substantial numbers (2–3.5 million) of governmental employees were counted as being unemployed. When a correct accounting is made for such persons, the pattern changes starkly to one of a rapid and continuous reduction in unemployment from 1932 until the recession of 1937–1938, which itself resulted from the Federal Reserve's doubling of reserve requirements between August 1936 and May 1937. This piece of detective work

no direct linkage between the overall or aggregate level of output and employment that would be determined by the attainment of equilibrium in labor and money markets and that level of output and employment that might be objectively considered desirable. In the actual equilibrium attained through the workings of the market process, persons might find themselves involuntarily unemployed, and they could not increase the overall level of employment by offers to work for lowered money wages. Nor could central bankers ensure a return to prosperity by the simple easing of money and credit markets. Under certain conditions, these actions could not reduce interest rates and, through this, increase the rate of capital investment. To shock the system out of its possible locked-in position, exogenous forces would have to be introduced, in the form of deficit spending by government.

The Birth of Macroeconomics

As if in one fell swoop, a new and exciting half-discipline was appended to the classical tradition. Macroeconomics was born almost full-blown from the Keynesian impact. To the conventional theory of resource allocation, now to be labeled "microeconomics," the new theory of employment was added, and labeled "macroeconomics." The professional economist, henceforward, would have to be trained in the understanding not only of the theory of the market process, but also the theory of aggregative economics, that theory from which predictions might be made about levels of employment and output. Even those who remained skeptical of the whole Keynesian edifice felt compelled to become expert in the manipulation of the conceptual models. And perhaps most importantly for our history, textbook writers responded by introducing simplistic Keynesian constructions into the elementary textbooks. Paul Samuelson's *Economics* (1948) swept the field, almost from its initial appearance early after the end of World War II. Other textbooks soon followed, and almost all were similar in their dichotomous presentation of subject matter. Courses were organized into two parts, microeconomics and

---

is due to Michael R. Darby, "Three-and-a-Half Million U.S. Employees Have Been Mislaid: Or, an Explanation of Unemployment, 1934–1941," *Journal of Political Economy* 84 (February 1976): 1–16.

macroeconomics, with relatively little concern about possible bridges between these sometimes disparate halves of the discipline.

Each part of the modified discipline carried with it implicit norms for social policy. Microeconomics, the rechristened traditional price theory, implicitly elevates allocative efficiency to a position as the dominant norm, and applications of theory here have usually involved demonstrations of the efficiency-producing or efficiency-retarding properties of particular institutional arrangements. Macroeconomics, the Keynesian consequence, elevates high-level output and employment to its position of normative dominance, with little or no indicated regard to the efficiency with which resources are utilized. There are, however, significant differences in the implications of these policy norms as between micro- and macroeconomics. In the former, the underlying ideal or optimum structure, toward which policy steps should legitimately be aimed, is a well-functioning regime of markets. At an analytical level, demonstrations that "markets fail" under certain conditions are taken to suggest that correctives will "make markets work" or, if this is impossible, will substitute regulation for markets, with the norm for regulation itself being that of duplicating market results. Equally, if not more, important are the demonstrations that markets fail because of unnecessary and inefficient political control and regulation, with the implication that removal and/or reduction of control itself will generate desired results. In summary, the policy implications of microeconomics are not themselves overtly interventionist and, if anything, probably tend toward the anti-interventionist pole.

The contrast with macroeconomics in this respect is striking. There is nothing akin to the "well-functioning market" which will produce optimally preferred results, no matter how well embedded in legal and institutional structure. Indeed, the central thrust of the Keynesian message is precisely to deny the existence of such an underlying ideal. "The economy," in the Keynesian paradigm, is afloat without a rudder, and its own internal forces, if left to themselves, are as likely to ground the system on the rocks of deep depression as they are to steer it toward the narrow channels of prosperity. Once this model for an economy is accepted to be analytically descriptive, even if major quibbles over details of interpretation persist, the overall direction of the economy by governmental or political control becomes almost morally imperative. There is a necessary interventionist bias which stems from the analytical basis of macroeconomics, a bias that is inherent in the paradigm itself and which need not be at all related to the ideological persuasion of the economist practitioner.

The New Role for the State

The Keynesian capture of the economists, therefore, carried with it a dramatically modified role for the state in their vision of the world. In this new vision, the state was obliged to take affirmative action toward ensuring that the national economy would remain prosperous, action which could, however, be taken with clearly defined objectives in view. Furthermore, in the initial surges of enthusiasm, few questions of conflict among objectives seemed to present themselves. Who could reject the desirability of high-level output and employment? Politicians responded quickly, and the effective "economic constitution" was changed to embody an explicit commitment of governmental responsibility for full employment. The Full Employment Act became law in the United States in 1946. The President's Council of Economic Advisers was created, reflecting the political recognition of the enhanced role of the economists and of economic theory after Keynes.[6]

The idealized scenario for the then "New Economics" was relatively straightforward. Economists were required first to make forecasts about the short- and medium-term movements in the appropriate aggregates—consumption, investment, public spending, and foreign trade. These forecasts were then to be fed into the suitably constructed model for the working of the national economy. Out of this, there was to emerge a prediction about equilibrium levels of output and employment. This prediction was then to be matched against desired or targeted values. If a shortfall seemed likely, further estimation was to be made about the required magnitude of adjustment. This result was then to be communicated to the decision makers, who would, presumably, respond by manipulating the government budget to accommodate the required changes.

This scenario, as sketched, encountered rough going early on when the immediate post–World War II forecasts proved so demonstrably in error.[7]

---

6. Stephen K. Bailey, *Congress Makes a Law* (New York: Columbia University Press, 1950), is the standard legislative history of the enactment of the Employment Act of 1946.

7. Such forecasts include S. Morris Livingston, "Forecasting Postwar Demand," *Econ-*

Almost from the onset of attempts to put Keynesian economics into practice, conflicts between the employment and the price-level objectives appeared, dousing the early enthusiasm for the economists' new Jerusalem. Nonetheless, there was no backtracking on the fundamental reassignment of functions. The responsibility for maintaining prosperity remained squarely on the shoulders of government. Stabilization policy occupied the minds and hearts of economists, even amidst the developing evidence of broad forecasting error, and despite the sharpening analytical criticism of the basic Keynesian structure. The newly acquired faith in macroeconomic policy tools was, in fact, maintained by the political lags in implementation. While textbooks spread the simple Keynesian precepts, and while learned academicians debated sophisticated points in logical analysis, the politics of policy proceeded much as before the revolution, enabling economists to blame government for observed stabilization failures. The recessions of the 1950s, even if mild by prewar standards, were held to reflect failures of political response. Economists in the academy were preparing the groundwork for the New Frontier, when Keynesian ideas shifted beyond the sanctuaries to capture the minds and hearts of ordinary politicians and the public.

The Scorn for Budget Balance

The old-time fiscal religion, which we have previously discussed in Chapter 2, was not easy to dislodge. Before the Keynesian challenge, an effective "fiscal constitution" did exist, even if this was not embodied in a written document. This "constitution" included the precept for budget balance, and this rule served as an important constraint on the natural proclivities of politicians. The economists who had absorbed the Keynesian teachings were faced with the challenge of persuading political leaders and the public at large that the old-time fiscal religion was irrelevant in the modern setting. As a sacrosanct principle, budget balance had to be uprooted. Prosperity in the na-

---

ometrica 13 (January 1945): 15–24; Richard A. Musgrave, "Alternative Budget Policies for Full Employment," *American Economic Review* 35 (June 1945): 387–400; National Planning Association, *National Budgets for Full Employment* (Washington: National Planning Association, 1945); and Arthur Smithies, "Forecasting Postwar Demand," *Econometrica* 13 (January 1945): 1–14. Such postwar forecasts were criticized in Albert G. Hart, " 'Model-Building' and Fiscal Policy," *American Economic Review* 35 (September 1945): 531–558.

tional economy, not any particular rule or state of the government's budget, was promoted as the overriding policy objective. And if the achievement and the maintenance of prosperity required deliberate creation of budget deficits, who should be concerned? Deficits in the government budget, said the Keynesians, were indeed small prices to pay for the blessings of high employment.

A new mythology was born. Since there was no particular virtue in budget balance, per se, there was no particular vice in budget unbalance, per se. The lesson was clear: Budget balance did not matter. There was apparently no normative relationship, even in some remote conceptual sense, between the two sides of the government's fiscal account. The government *was* different from the individual. The Keynesian-oriented textbooks hammered home this message to a continuing sequence of student cohort groups. Is there any wonder that, eventually, the message would be heeded?

The New Precepts for Fiscal Policy

The new rules that were to guide fiscal policy were simple. Budget deficits were to be created when aggregate demand threatened to fall short of that level required to maintain full employment. Conversely, and symmetrically, budget surpluses were to be created when aggregate demand threatened to exceed full-employment targets, generating price inflation. A balanced budget would rationally emerge only when aggregate demand was predicted to be just sufficient to generate full employment without exerting inflationary pressures on prices. Otherwise, unbalanced budgets would be required. In this pure regime of functional finance, a regime in which the government's budget was to be used, and used rationally, as the primary instrument for stabilization, budget deficits or budget surpluses might emerge over some cumulative multiperiod sequence. Those who were most explicit in their advocacy of such a regime expressed little or no concern for the direction of budget unbalance over time.[8] In the wake of the experience of the Great Depression, however, the emphasis was placed on the possible need for a continuing sequence of deficits. The potential application of the new fiscal principles in

8. The clearest exposition of a position that was widely shared is found in Abba P. Lerner, *The Economics of Control* (New York: Macmillan, 1944), pp. 285–322.

threatened inflationary periods was discussed largely in hypothetical terms, appended to lend analytical symmetry to the policy models.

Budget Deficits, Public Debt, and Money Creation

The deliberate creation of budget deficits—the explicit decision to spend and not to tax—was the feature of Keynesian policy that ran most squarely in the face of traditional and time-honored norms for fiscal responsibility. But there was no alternative for the Keynesian convert. To increase aggregate demand, total spending in the economy must be increased, and this could only be guaranteed if the private-spending offsets of tax increase could be avoided or swamped. New net spending must emerge, and the creation of budget deficits offered the only apparent escape from economic stagnation.[9]

If, however, the flow of spending was to be increased in this manner, the problem of financing deficits necessarily arose. And at this point, the policy advocate encountered two separate and subsidiary norms in the previously existing "constitution." Deficits could be financed in only one of two ways, either through government borrowing (the issue of public debt) or through the explicit creation of money (available only to central government). But public debt, in the classical theory of public finance, transfers burdens onto the shoulders of future generations. And money creation was associated, historically, with governmental corruption along with the dangers of inflation.

Retrospectively, it remains somewhat surprising that the Keynesians, or most of them, chose to challenge the debt-burden argument of classical public-finance theory rather than the money-creation alternative. (By so doing, quite unnecessary intellectual confusion was introduced into an important area of economic theory, confusion that had not, even as late as 1976, been fully eliminated.) Within the strict assumptions of the Keynesian model, and in the deficient-demand setting, the opportunity cost of additional gov-

---

9. For completeness, we should note here that the Keynesian theory of policy, as developed in the 1940s and 1950s, included the balanced-budget multiplier. Aggregate spending in the economy might be increased by an increase in government outlays, even if budget balance is strictly maintained, because of the fact that the increased tax revenues would be drawn, in part, from private savings. The standard exposition of this proposition is William J. Baumol and Maurice H. Peston, "More on the Multiplier Effects of a Balanced Budget," *American Economic Review* 45 (March 1955): 140–148.

ernmental spending is genuinely zero. From this, it follows directly that the creation of money to finance the required deficit involves no net cost; there is no danger of price inflation. In the absence of political-institutional constraints, therefore, the idealized Keynesian policy package for escape from such economic situations is the explicit creation of budget deficits along with the financing of these by pure money issue.

In such a context, any resort to public debt issue, to public borrowing, is a necessary second-best. Why should the government offer any interest return at all to potential lenders of funds, to the purchasers of government debt instruments, when the alternative of printing money at negligible real cost and at zero interest is available? Regardless of the temporal location of the burden of servicing and amortizing public debt, there is no supportable argument for public borrowing in the setting of deficient demand. In trying to work out a supporting argument here, the Keynesian economists were confused, even on their own terms.

Because they unreasonably assumed that deficits were to be financed by public borrowing rather than by money creation, the Keynesian advocates felt themselves obliged to reduce the sting of the argument concerning the temporal transfer of cost or burden.[10] To accomplish this, they revived in sophisticated form the distinction between the norms for private, personal financial integrity and those for public, governmental financial responsibility. Budget balance did matter for an individual or family; budget balance did not matter for a government. Borrowing for an individual offered a means of postponing payment, of putting off the costs of current spending, which might or might not be desirable. For government, however, there was no such temporal transfer. It was held to be impossible to implement a transfer of cost or burden through time because government included all members of the community, and, so long as public debt was internally owned, "we owe it to ourselves." Debtors and creditors were mutually canceling; hence, in the macroeconomic context, the society could never be "in debt" in any way

---

10. Richard A. Musgrave, in reviewing Alvin Hansen's role in the selling of Keynesianism in the 1940s, acknowledged the pivotal position occupied by the classical theory of public debt when he wrote: "The battle for full employment had to be continued, and the counteroffensive, built around the alleged dangers of a rising public debt, had to be met." See Musgrave's contribution to the symposium on Alvin H. Hansen: "Caring for the Real Problems," *Quarterly Journal of Economics* 90 (February 1976): 5.

comparable to that situation in which a person, a family, a firm, a local government, or even a central government that had borrowed from foreigners might find itself.

This argument was deceptively attractive. It did much to remove the charge of fiscal irresponsibility from the deficit-creation position. Politicians and the public might hold fast to the classical theory, in its vulgar or its sophisticated variant, but so long as professional economists could be found to present the plausible counterargument, this flank of the Keynesian intellectual position was amply protected, or so it seemed.

The "new orthodoxy" of public debt stood almost unchallenged among economists during the 1940s and 1950s, despite its glaring logical contradictions.[11] The Keynesian advocates failed to see that, if their theory of debt burden is correct, the benefits of public spending are always available without cost merely by resort to borrowing, and without regard to the phase of the economic cycle. If there is no transfer of cost onto taxpayers in future periods (whether these be the same or different from current taxpayers), and if bond purchasers voluntarily transfer funds to government in exchange for promises of future interest and amortization payments, there is no cost to anyone in society at the time public spending is carried out. Only the benefits of such spending remain. The economic analogue to the perpetual motion machine would have been found.

A central confusion in the whole Keynesian argument lay in its failure to bring policy alternatives down to the level of choices confronted by individual citizens, or confronted for them by their political representatives, and, in turn, to predict the effects of these alternatives on the utilities of individuals.

---

11. The "new orthodoxy" was first challenged explicitly by James M. Buchanan in 1958. In his book, *Public Principles of Public Debt* (Homewood, Ill.: Richard D. Irwin, 1958), Buchanan specifically refuted the three main elements of the Keynesian theory, and he argued that, in its essentials, the pre-Keynesian classical theory of public debt was correct. Buchanan's thesis was widely challenged and a lively debate among economists took place in the early 1960s. Many of the contributions are included in James M. Ferguson, ed., *Public Debt and Future Generations* (Chapel Hill: University of North Carolina Press, 1964). For a summary treatment, see James M. Buchanan and Richard E. Wagner, *Public Debt in a Democratic Society* (Washington: American Enterprise Institute, 1967). Buchanan sought to place elements of the debt-burden discussion in a broader framework of economic theory in his book, *Cost and Choice* (Chicago: Markham, 1968). For a later paper that places the debt-burden discussion in a cost-theory perspective, see E. G. West, "Public Debt Burden and Cost Theory," *Economic Inquiry* 13 (June 1975): 179–190.

It proved difficult to get at, and to correct, this fundamental confusion because of careless and sloppy usage of institutional description. The Keynesian economist rarely made the careful distinction between money creation and public debt issue that is required as the first step toward logical clarity. Linguistically, he often referred to what amounts to disguised money creation as "public debt," notably in his classification of government "borrowing" from the banking system. He tended to equate the whole defense of deficit financing with his defense of public debt, as a financing instrument, when, as noted above, this need not have been done at all. On his own grounds, the Keynesian economist could have made a much more effective case for deficit financing by direct money creation. Had he done so, perhaps the transmission of his message to the politicians and to the public would have contained within it much stronger built-in safeguards. It is indeed interesting to speculate what might have happened in the post-Keynesian world of fiscal policy if the financing of budget deficits had been restricted to money issue, and if this means of financing had been explicitly acknowledged by all parties.

The Dreams of Camelot

But such was not to be. The Keynesian economists were able to remain within their ivory towers during the 1950s, secure in their own untested confusions and willingly assessing blame upon the mossback attitudes of politicians and the public. In the early 1960s, for a few months in history, all their dreams seemed to become potentially realizable. The "New Economics" had finally moved beyond the elementary textbooks and beyond the halls of the academy. The enlightened would rule the world, or at least the economic aspects of it. But such dreams of Camelot, in economic policy as in other areas, were dashed against the hard realities of democratic politics. Institutional constraints, which seem so commonplace to the observer of the 1970s, were simply overlooked by the Keynesian economists until these emerged so quickly in the 1960s. They faced the rude awakening to the simple fact that their whole analytical structure, its strengths and its weaknesses, had been constructed and elaborated in almost total disregard for the institutional world where decisions are and must be made. The political history of economic policy for the 1960s and 1970s, which we shall trace further in Chapter 4, is not a happy one. Can we seriously absolve the academic scribblers from their own share of blame?

4. The Spread of the New Gospel

Introduction

Economists do not control political history, despite their desires and dreams. Our narrative summary of the Keynesian revolution cannot, therefore, be limited to the conversion of the economists. We must look at the spreading of the Keynesian gospel to the public, and especially to the political decision makers, if we are to make sense of the situation that we confront in the late 1970s and the 1980s. The old-time fiscal religion was surprisingly strong. The effective fiscal constitution was not amended at one fell swoop, and not without some struggle. But ultimately it did give way; its precepts lost their power of persuasion. The Keynesian revolution began in the classroom and was nurtured there, but ultimately it invaded the citadels of power. The ideas of the Cambridge academic scribbler did modify, and profoundly, the actions of politicians, and with precisely the sort of time lag that Keynes himself noted in the very last paragraph of his book. Since the early 1960s, politicians have become at least half Keynesians, or they have done so in sufficient number to ensure that budget policy proceeds from a half-Keynesian paradigm. We shall discuss the attitudes of modern politicians at length, but we must first complete our narrative.

Passive Imbalance

Budget deficits may emerge either as a result of deliberate decisions to spend beyond ordinary revenue constraints or because established flows of spending and taxing react differently to shifts in the aggregate bases of an economy. We may refer to these as "active" and "passive" deficits, respectively. One of the first effects of the Great Depression of the 1930s, which dramatically reduced income, output, and employment in the American economy, was the generation of a deficit in the federal government's budget. From a position of comfortable surplus in 1929, the budget became unbalanced in calendar 1930, largely owing to the dramatic reduction in tax revenues. This revenue shortfall, plus the increase in transfer programs, created an even larger deficit for 1931.

The old-time fiscal religion, which embodied the analogy between private and public finance, dictated revenue-increasing and spending-decreasing actions as countermeasures to the emergence of passive budget deficits. These precepts were dominant in 1932 when, in reaction to the deficits of the two preceding calendar years, along with prospects for even larger deficits, federal taxes were increased substantially.[1] Even this tax increase was apparently not sufficient to stifle political criticism; Franklin D. Roosevelt based his electoral campaign of 1932 on a balanced-budget commitment, and he severely criticized Herbert Hoover for the fiscal irresponsibility that the budget deficits reflected. In a radio address in July 1932, for instance, Roosevelt said, "Let us have the courage to stop borrowing to meet continuing deficits. . . . Revenues must cover expenditures by one means or another. Any government, like any family, can, for a year, spend a little more than it earns. But you and I know that a continuation of that habit means the poorhouse."[2]

The first task for the economists, even in these years before the publication of Keynes' book, seemed to be clear. They tried, or at least many of them did, to convince President Roosevelt, along with other political leaders, that the emerging budget deficits, passively and indirectly created, gave no cause for alarm, and that tax increases and spending cuts could only be counterproductive in the general restoration of prosperity.[3] Once in office, President Roosevelt soon found that, regardless of the old-fashioned precepts discussed in his campaign, expansions in spending programs were politically popular, while tax increases were not. So long as the traditional rules were not widely

1. For a general discussion of fiscal policy in the 1930s, with an emphasis on the effects of the tax increase of 1932, see E. C. Brown, "Fiscal Policy in the Thirties: A Reappraisal," *American Economic Review* 46 (December 1956): 857–879.

2. Cited in Fredrick C. Mosher and Orville F. Poland, *The Costs of American Government* (New York: Dodd, Mead, 1964), p. 73.

3. For a discussion of the attitudes of American economists in the early 1930s, particularly those associated with the University of Chicago, see J. Ronnie Davis, *The New Economics and the Old Economists* (Ames: Iowa State University Press, 1971).

violated, so long as the times could genuinely be judged extraordinary, and so long as there were economists around to offer plausible reasons for allowing the emerging deficits to go undisturbed, political decision makers were ready to oblige, even if they continued to pay lip service to the old-time principles.

Even before 1936, therefore, the first step on the road toward political implementation of the full Keynesian message was accomplished. During periods of economic distress, when the maintenance of budget balance required explicit action toward increasing taxes and/or reducing governmental outlays, the political weakness inherent in the traditional fiscal constitution was exposed, and the norms were violated with little observable consequence. Until Keynes presented his "General Theory," however, these policy actions (or inactions) were not embedded in a normative analytical framework that elevated the budget itself to a dominant instrumental role in maintaining prosperity. The basic Keynesian innovation lay precisely in such explicit use of the budget for this purpose, one that had scarcely been dreamed of in any pre-Keynesian philosophy.[4] As we have noted, many economists readily accepted the new religion. But the conversion of the politicians encountered unpredicted obstacles.

In the euphoria of victory in World War II, and flush with the observed faith of economists in their new prophet, the Full Employment Act of 1946 became law. Despite the vagueness of its objectives, this act seemed to reflect an acceptance of governmental responsibility for the maintenance of economic prosperity, and it seemed also to offer economists an opportunity to demonstrate their greatly enhanced social productivity. Early expectations were rudely shattered, however, by the abject failure of the Keynesian economic forecasters in the immediate postwar years. The initial bloom of Keynesian hopes faded, and politicians and the public adopted a cautious wait-and-see attitude toward macroeconomic policy planning.

---

4. Gottfried Haberler observed, with reference to Keynes, that "no 'classical' economist had propagated the case for easy money and deficit spending with the same energy, persuasiveness, and enthusiasm as Keynes, and with the seemingly general theoretical underpinning, and that many orthodox economists rejected these policies outright." See Haberler's contribution to the symposium on Alvin H. Hansen: "Some Reminiscences," *Quarterly Journal of Economics* 90 (February 1976): 11.

Built-in Flexibility

The late 1940s saw many of the Keynesian economists licking their wounds, resting content with the exposition of the Keynesian message in the elementary textbooks, and taking initial steps toward consolidating the territory staked out in the 1930s. The apparent coolness of the politicians toward the active creation of budget deficits, along with the economists' own forecasting limits, suggested that more effective use might be made of the observed political acquiescence to passive imbalance. Even if budget deficits could not be, or would not be, created explicitly for the attainment of desired macroeconomic objectives, the two sides of the budget might be evaluated, at least in part, according to their by-product effects in furthering these objectives. If the politicians could be brought to this level of economic sophistication, a second major step toward the Keynesian policy mecca would have been taken. The initial assurance against reactions toward curing passive imbalance would now be supplemented by political recognition that the budget deficit, in itself, worked as a major element toward restoring prosperity. For the politicians to deplore the fiscal irresponsibility reflected in observed deficits while passively accepting these and foregoing counterproductive fiscal measures was one thing; for these same politicians to recognize that the observed deficits themselves offered one means of returning the economy toward desired output and employment levels was quite another.

Once the emergence of deficits came to be viewed as a corrective force, and once alternative budgets came to be evaluated by the strength of the corrective potential, only a minor shift in attitude was required to incorporate such potential in the objectives for budget making itself. The economists quickly inserted "built-in flexibility" as a norm for both the taxing and spending sides of the fiscal account. Other things equal, taxes "should" be levied so as to ensure wide variations in revenue over the business cycle, variations that carry the same sign as those in the underlying economic aggregates, and which are disproportionately larger than the latter. Similarly, for the other side of the budget, spending programs, and notably transfers, "should" be arranged so that variations over the cycle are of the opposing sign to those in the underlying economic aggregates and, ideally, of disproportionate magnitude. These post-Keynesian norms for the internal structure of budget making offered support to those political pressures which would ordinarily support progressive taxation of personal incomes, along with the taxation of corporate income and/or profits, and, on the spending side, the initiation or increase of welfare-type transfers.[5]

Hypothetical Budget Balance

Even with passive imbalance accepted, however, and even with built-in flexibility accorded some place in an array of fiscal norms, a major step in the political conversion to Keynesian economics remained to be accomplished. Balance or imbalance in the budget was still related to income, output, and employment only in some *ex post* sense. The specific relationship between budget balance, per se, and the level of national income was not developed in the early discussions among the fiscal policy economists and surely not in the thinking of political leaders. In its early formulations, Keynesian fiscal policy involved the deliberate usage of the budget to achieve desired levels of income and employment, the use of "functional finance," without regard to the question of balance or imbalance. And, indeed, much of the early discussion implied that a regime of permanent and continuing budget deficits would be required to ensure economic prosperity.

As the predictions of events for 1946 and 1947 turned sour, however, and as inflation rather than stagnation appeared as an unanticipated problem for the American economy, the question of budget balance more or less naturally presented itself. Even the most ardent Keynesian could not legitimately support the creation of budget deficits in periods of full employment and high national income. In other words, the budget "should" attain balance once the macroeconomic objectives desired are attained. This conclusion provided, in its turn, a norm for directly relating the degree of balance or imbalance in the government's budget to the underlying state of the economy.

The limitations on forecasting ability, along with the political-institutional constraints on discretionary budgetary adjustments, turned attention to built-in flexibility. It was suggested that, with such flexibility, the Keynesian policy norms could be applied even in the restrictive setting of passive imbalance.

---

5. For an early analysis, see Richard A. Musgrave and Merton H. Miller, "Built-in Flexibility," *American Economic Review* 38 (March 1948): 122–128.

If political decision makers either would not or could not manipulate the two sides of the budget so as to further output and employment objectives directly, the Keynesian precepts still might prove of value in determining long-range targets for budget planning. The economists still might have something to offer. When should the government's budget be balanced? When should planned rates of outlay be fully covered by anticipated revenue streams? The post-Keynesians had clear answers. Both the expenditure and the tax side of the budget should be arranged, on a quasipermanent basis, so that overall balance would be achieved if and when certain output and employment objectives were attained.

Budget balance at some hypothetical level of national income, as opposed to any balance between observed revenue and spending flows, became the norm for quasipermanent changes in taxes and expenditures. Proposals for implementing this notion of hypothetical budget balance were specifically made in 1947 by the Committee for Economic Development.[6] In 1948, the proposal was elaborated in a more sophisticated form by Milton Friedman.[7] Professional economists attained a "remarkable degree of consensus" in support of the norm of hypothetical budget balance in the late 1940s and early 1950s.[8]

Monetary Policy and Inflation

The economists' discussions of built-in flexibility and of budget balance at some hypothetical level of national income stemmed from two separate sources. The first, as noted above, was the recognition that discretionary budget management simply was not within the spirit of the times. The second, and equally important, source of the newfound emphasis lay in the dra-

---

6. Committee for Economic Development, *Taxes and the Budget: A Program for Prosperity in a Free Economy* (New York: Committee for Economic Development, 1947). This proposal, along with the intellectual antecedents, is discussed in Walter W. Heller, "CED's Stabilizing Budget Policy after Ten Years," *American Economic Review* 47 (September 1957): 634–651.

7. Milton Friedman, "A Monetary and Fiscal Framework for Economic Stability," *American Economic Review* 48 (June 1948): 245–264.

8. For a summary discussion, see Heller. It should be noted that Heller distinguished between a "tranquilizing budget policy" and a "stabilizing budget policy," and threw his support to the latter.

matically modified historical setting. Keynesian economics, and the policy precepts it embodied, was developed almost exclusively in application to a depressed national economy, with high unemployment, excess industrial capacity, and little or no upward pressures on prices. But the years after World War II were, by contrast, years of rapidly increasing output, near full employment, and inflationary movements in prices.

The Keynesian elevation of the budget to its position as the dominant instrument for macroeconomic policy, along with the parallel relegation of monetary policy to a subsidiary role, was based, in large part, on the alleged presence of a liquidity trap during periods of deep depression. The basic model was asymmetrical, however, for nothing in Keynesian analysis suggested that monetary controls could not be effectively applied to dampen inflationary threats. Properly interpreted, Keynesian analysis does not imply that money does not matter; it implies that money matters asymmetrically. High interest rates offer, in this analysis, one means of choking off an inflationary boom. But this policy instrument need not be dusted off and utilized if, in fact, fiscal policy precepts are adhered to, in boom times as well as bust.

Immediately after World War II, the Keynesian economists came close to convincing the Truman-era politicians that a permanent regime of low interest rates, of "easy money," could at long last be realized. But the fiscal counterpart to such an "easy money" regime, one that required the accumulation of budgetary surpluses, did not readily come into being. As the inflationary threat seemed to worsen, money and monetary control were rediscovered in practice in 1951, along with the incorporation of a policy asymmetry into the discussions and the textbooks of the time. "You can't push on a string"—this analogy suggested that monetary policy was an appropriate instrument for restricting total spending but inappropriate for expanding it.

This one-sided incorporation of monetary policy instruments makes difficult our attempt to trace the conversion of politicians to Keynesian ideas. Without the dramatic shift in the potential for monetary policy that came with the Treasury–Federal Reserve Accord in 1951, we might simply look at the record for the Eisenhower years to determine the extent to which the Keynesian fiscal policy precepts were honored. But the shift did occur, and there need have been nothing specifically "non-Keynesian" about using the policy instruments asymmetrically over the cycle. A regime with alternating periods of "easy budgets and tight money" suggested a way station between the rhetoric of the old-time fiscal religion and the Keynesian spree of the 1960s and 1970s.

The Rhetoric and the Reality of the Fifties

How are we to classify the Eisenhower years? Did the fiscal politics of the 1950s fully reflect Keynesian teachings? Politically, should we call these years "pre-Keynesian" or "post-Keynesian"?

The answers must be ambiguous for several reasons. The relatively mild swings in the business cycle offered us no definitive test of political will. There is nothing in the historical record that demonstrates a political willingness to use the budget actively as an instrument for securing and maintaining high-level employment and output. On the other hand, the record does show a willingness to acquiesce in passive budget imbalance, along with repeated commitments for explicit utilization of budgetary instruments in the event of serious economic decline. The political economics of the Eisenhower years was clearly not that of the 1960s, which we can definitely label as "post-Keynesian," but it was far from the economics of the 1920s.

Much of the rhetoric was pre-Keynesian, both with specific reference to budget balance and with reference to other macroeconomic concerns. The conflict between the high-employment and price-level objectives, a conflict that was obscured in the Great Depression only to surface with a vengeance in the late 1940s, divided the most ardent Keynesians and their opponents. The former, almost without exception, tended to place high employment at the top of their priority listing, and to neglect the dangers of inflation. Those who were most reluctant to embrace Keynesian policy norms took the opposing stance and indicated a willingness to accept lower levels of employment in exchange for a more secure throttle on inflation. The Eisenhower administration came into office with an expressed purpose of doing something about the inflation of the postwar years, and also about a parallel policy target, the growth in the rate of federal spending. A modified trade-off among macroeconomic objectives, quite apart from an acceptance and understanding of the Keynesian policy instruments, would have been sufficient to explain the observed behavior of the Eisenhower political leaders. That is to say, the politicians of the 1950s, on the basis of their observed actions alone, cannot be found guilty of pre-Keynesian ignorance. They were, of course, sharply criticized by the "Keynesians"; but this criticism was centered more on the acknowledged value trade-off between the inflation and unemployment targets than the use or misuse of the policy instruments.

At a different level of assessment, however, we must look at the analytical presuppositions of these decision makers. Did they acknowledge the existence of the trade-off between employment and inflation, the trade-off that was almost universally accepted and widely discussed by the economists of the decade? Was the Eisenhower economic policy based on an explicit willingness to tolerate somewhat higher rates of unemployment than might have been possible in exchange for a somewhat more stable level of prices? If the evidence suggests an affirmative answer, we may say that the political conversion to Keynesian economics was instrumentally completed. We are, of course, economists, and it is all too easy to interpret and to explain the events of history "as if" the results emerge from economists' models. It is especially tempting to explain the macroeconomics of the 1950s in such terms and to say that the Eisenhower political leaders were dominated by a fear of inflation while remaining relatively unconcerned about unemployment.

If we look again at the rhetoric of the 1950s, along with the reality, however, and if we try to do so without wearing the economists' blinders, the label "pre-Keynesian" fits the Eisenhower politicians better than does its opposite. The paradigm of the decade was that of an economic system that is inherently stable, provided that taxes are not onerously high and government spending is not out of bounds, and provided that the central bank carries out its appropriate monetary role. There was no political inclination to use the federal budget for achieving some hypothetical and targeted rate of growth in national income. The economics of George Humphrey and Robert Anderson was little different from that of Andrew Mellon, thirty years before.[9] The economics of the economists was, of course, dramatically different. In the 1920s, there was no overt policy conflict between the economists and the

---

9. In his book, *Taxation: The People's Business* (New York: Macmillan, 1924), Mellon not only noted that "the government is just a business, and can and should be run on business principles . . ." (p. 17), but also remarked approvingly that "since the war two guiding principles have dominated the financial policy of the Government. One is the balancing of the budget, and the other is the payment of the public debt. Both are in line with the fundamental policy of the Government since its beginning" (p. 25).

politicians of their time. By contrast, the 1950s were years of developing tension between the economists-intellectuals and their political peers, with the Keynesian economists unceasingly berating the effective decision makers for their failure to have learned the Keynesian lessons, for their reactionary adherence to outmoded principles of fiscal rectitude. This discourse laid the groundwork for the policy shift of the 1960s.

But, as noted earlier, there were major differences between the 1920s and the 1950s. Passive deficits were accepted, even if there was extreme reluctance to utilize the budget actively to combat what proved to be relatively mild swings in the aggregate economy. The built-in flexibility embodied in the federal government's budget was both acknowledged and allowed to work. Furthermore, despite the rhetoric that called for the accumulation of budget surpluses during periods of economic recovery, little or no action was taken to ensure that sizeable surpluses did, in fact, occur. The promised increased flow of revenues was matched by commitments for new spending, and the Eisenhower leadership did not effectively forestall this. Public debt was not reduced in any way remotely comparable to the previous postwar periods.

Fiscal Drag

The Eisenhower administration was most severely criticized for its failure to pursue an active fiscal policy during and after the 1958 recession. Political pressures for quick tax reduction were contained in 1958, with the assistance of Democratic leaders in Congress, and attempts were made to convert the massive $12 billion passive deficit of that year into budget surpluses for the recovery years, 1959 and 1960. The rate of growth in federal spending was held down, and a relatively quick turnaround in the impact of the budget on the national economy was achieved, in the face of continuing high levels of unemployment.

It was during these last months of the Eisenhower administration that the notion or concept of "fiscal drag" emerged in the policy discourse of economists, based on an extension and elaboration of the norm for budget balance at some hypothetically defined level of national income and incorporating the recognition that income grows through time. The Eisenhower budgetary policy for the recovery years of 1959 and 1960 was sharply criticized for its apparent concentration on observed rather than potential flows of revenues and outlays. By defining a target "high-employment" level of national income on a projected normal growth path, and then by projecting and estimating the tax revenues and government outlays that would be forthcoming under existing programs at that level of income, a test for hypothetical budget balance could be made. Preliminary tests suggested that the Eisenhower budgetary policies for those years would have generated a surplus at the targeted high-employment level of income. That is to say, although actually observed flows of revenues and outlays need not have indicated a budget surplus, such a surplus would indeed have been created if national income had been generated at the higher and more desired level. However, since observed national income was below this target level, and because the potential for the surplus was already incorporated in the tax-spending structure, the budget instrument itself worked against the prospect that the target level of national income could ever be attained at all. This result seemed to follow directly from the recognition that the budget itself was an important determinant of national income. Before the targeted level of income could be reached, the budget itself would begin to exert a depressing influence on aggregate demand. This "fiscal drag" was something to be avoided.[10]

From this analysis follows the budgetary precept that runs so strongly counter to ordinary common sense. During a period of economic recovery, the deliberate creation of a budget deficit, or the creation of a larger deficit than might already exist, offers a means of securing the achievement of budget surplus at high-employment income. We shall discuss this argument further at a later point. But here we note only that this was the prevailing wisdom among the enlightened economists on the Washington scene in 1960; this, plus the relatively sluggish recovery itself, provided the setting for the politics and the economics of Kennedy's New Frontier.

10. The interest in revenue sharing that surfaced in the early 1960s was, at that time, sparked in part by a desire to offset fiscal drag. Rather than cutting taxes to avoid fiscal drag, it was proposed that revenues be transferred to state and local governments. For references to what, at the time, was referred to as the "Heller-Pechman proposal," see Walter W. Heller, "Strengthening the Fiscal Base of Our Federalism," in *New Dimensions of Political Economy* (Cambridge: Harvard University Press, 1966), pp. 117–172; and Joseph A. Pechman, "Financing State and Local Government," in *Proceedings of a Symposium on Federal Taxation* (New York: American Bankers Association, 1965), pp. 71–85.

The Reluctant Politician

In one of his more exuberant moments, President Kennedy may have called himself a Berliner; but during the early months of his administration, he could scarcely have called himself a Keynesian. As Herbert Stein suggested, "Kennedy's fiscal thinking was conventional. He believed in budget-balancing. While he was aware of circumstances in which the budget could not or should not be balanced, he preferred a balanced budget, being in this respect like most other people but unlike modern economists."[11] But President Kennedy's economic advisers were, to a man, solidly Keynesian, in both the instrumental and the valuational meaning of this term. They were willing to recommend the usage of the full array of budgetary instruments to secure high employment and economic growth, and they were relatively unconcerned about the inflationary danger that such policies might produce. The trade-off between employment and inflation was explicitly incorporated in their models of economic process, and they were willing to accept the relatively limited inflation that these models seemed to suggest as the price for higher employment.

But these advisers were also Galbraithian, in that they preferred to increase demand through expansions in federal spending rather than through tax reductions. Furthermore, they were strongly supportive of "easy money," a policy of low interest rates designed to stimulate domestic investment. These patterns of adjustment were closely attuned with the standard political pressures upon the Democratic administration. Hence, in 1961 and early 1962, there was little or no discussion of tax reduction, despite the continuing sluggishness of the national economy, sluggishness that was still blamed on the follies of the previous Eisenhower leadership. Balance-of-payments difficulties prevented the adoption of the monetary policy that the Keynesians desired, and dramatic proposals for large increases in federal spending would

---

11. Herbert Stein, *The Fiscal Revolution in America* (Chicago: University of Chicago Press, 1969), p. 375. We should acknowledge our indebtedness to Stein's careful and complete history of fiscal policy over the whole post-Keynesian period before the late 1960s. Our interpretation differs from that advanced by Stein largely in the fact that we have had an additional decade in which to evaluate the record, the events of which have done much to reduce the faith of economists, regardless of their ideological persuasion, in the basic Keynesian precepts.

surely have run squarely in the face of congressional opposition, a fact that President Kennedy fully recognized. Stimulation of the economy was, therefore, limited in total, despite the arguments of the president's advisers.

Political Keynesianism: The Tax Cut of 1964

The principles of the old-fashioned fiscal religion did not remain inviolate up until the early 1960s only to collapse under the renewed onslaught of the modern economists. The foundations had been eroded, gradually and inexorably, since the conversion of the economists in the 1940s. And the political resistance to an activist fiscal policy was steadily weakened throughout the 1950s, despite much rhetoric to the contrary. But if a single event must be chosen to mark the full political acceptance of the Keynesian policy gospel, the tax cut of 1964 stands alone. Initially discussed in 1962, actively proposed and debated throughout 1963, and finally enacted in early 1964, this tax reduction demonstrated that political decision makers could act, and did act, to use the federal budget in an effort to achieve a hypothetical target for national income. Tax rates were reduced, and substantially so, despite the presence of an existing budget deficit, and despite the absence of economic recession. The argument for this unprecedented step was almost purely Keynesian. There was little recourse to the Mellon-Taft-Humphrey view that lowered tax rates, whenever and however implemented, offered the sure path to prosperity. Instead, taxes were to be reduced because national income was not being generated at a level that was potentially attainable, given the resource capacities of the nation. The economy was growing, but not nearly fast enough, and the increased deficit resulting from the tax cut was to be the instrument that moved the economy to its growth path. There was no parallel reformist argument for expenditure increase, and the tax reduction in itself was not wildly redistributionist. The objective was clean and simple: the restoration of the national economy to its full growth potential.

Should we not have predicted that the economists would be highly pleased in their newly established positions? The "New Economics" had, at long last, arrived; the politicians had finally been converted; the Keynesian revolution had become reality; its principles were henceforward to be enshrined in the conventional political wisdom. These were truly the economists' halcyon days.

But days they were, or perhaps months. How can they (we) have been so naive? This question must have emerged to plague those who were most enthusiastic, and it must have done so soon after 1965. Could the fiscal politics of the next decade, 1965–1975, and beyond, not have been foreseen, predicted, and possibly forestalled? Or did the economists in Camelot dream of a future in which democratic fiscal politics were to be replaced, once and for all, by the fiscal gospel of Lord Keynes, as amended? We shall discuss such questions in depth, but for now we emphasize only the results of this conversion of the politicians to the Keynesian norms. As we have pointed out, this conversion was a gradual one, extending over the several decades, but 1964–1965 offers the historical watershed. Before this date, the fiscal politics of America was at least partially "pre-Keynesian" in both rhetoric and reality. After 1965, the fiscal politics became definitely "post-Keynesian" in reality, although elements of the old-time religion remained in the political argument.

The results are on record for all to see. After 1964, the United States embarked on a course of fiscal irresponsibility matched by no other period in its two-century history. A record-setting deficit of $25 billion in 1968 generated a temporary obeisance to the old-fashioned verities in 1969, the first Nixon year. But following this, the federal government's budget swept onward and upward toward explosive heights, financed increasingly and disproportionately by deficits. Deficits of more than $23 billion were recorded in each of the 1971 and 1972 fiscal years. This provided the setting for Nixon's putative 1974 "battle of the budget," his last pre-Watergate scandal effort to bring spending into line with revenues. Fiscal 1973 saw the deficit reduced to plausibly acceptable limits, only to become dangerously large in fiscal 1975 and 1976, when a two-year deficit of more than $100 billion was accumulated. Who can look into our fiscal future without trepidation, regardless of his own political or ideological persuasion?

The mystery lies not in the facts of the fiscal record, but in the failure of social scientists, and economists in particular, to predict the results of the eclipse of the old rules for fiscal responsibility. Once democratically elected politicians, and behind them their constituents in the voting public, were finally convinced that budget balance carried little or no normative weight, what was there left to restrain the ever-present spending pressures? The results are, and should have been, predictable at the most naive level of behavioral analysis. We shall examine this failure of prediction in Part II, but the facts suggest that the naive analysis would have been applicable. After the

1964 tax reduction, the "price" of public goods and services seemed lower. Should we not have foreseen efforts to "purchase" larger quantities? Should we not have predicted the Great Society–Viet Nam spending explosion of the late 1960s?

Economists, Politicians, and the Public

The Keynesian economists are ready with responses to such questions. They fall back on the symmetrical applicability of the basic Keynesian policy precepts, and they lay the fiscal-monetary irresponsibility squarely on the politicians. If the political decision makers of the 1960s and 1970s, exemplified particularly in Lyndon Johnson and Richard Nixon (both of whom remain forever villains in the liberal intellectuals' lexicon), had listened to the advice of their economist advisers, as did their counterparts in Camelot, the economic disasters need not have emerged. After all, or so the argument of the Keynesian economists proceeds, the precepts are wholly symmetrical. Budget surpluses may be desired at certain times. Enlightened political leadership would have imposed higher taxes after 1965, as their economist advisers recommended, and efforts would have been made to hold down rates of growth in federal domestic spending to offset Viet Nam outlays.

In such attempts to evade their own share of the responsibility for the post-1965 fiscal history, the economists rarely note the politician's place in a democratic society. From Roosevelt's New Deal onward, elected politicians have lived with the demonstrated relationship between favorable election returns and expansion in public spending programs. Can anyone seriously expect the ordinary persons who are elected to office to act differently from the rest of us? The only effective constraint on the spending proclivities of elected politicians from the 1930s onward has been the heritage of our historical "fiscal constitution," a set of rules that did include the balancing of outlays with revenues. But once this constraint was eliminated, why should the elected politician behave differently from the way we have observed him to behave after 1965? Could we have expected the president and the Congress, Democratic or Republican, to propose and to enact significant tax-rate increases during a period of economic prosperity? In Camelot, the politicians followed the economists' advice because such advice coincided directly with the naturally emergent political pressures. Why did the economists fail to see that a setting in which the appropriate Keynesian policy would run directly counter to these natural pressures might generate quite different results?

Functional Finance and Hypothetical Budget Balance

In retrospect, it may be argued that damage was done to the basic Keynesian cause by the attempts to provide substitutes for the balanced-budget rule, and most notably by the rule that the government's budget "should" be balanced at some hypothetical level of national income, a level that describes full capacity or full-employment output. In the pristine simplicity of their early formulation, most clearly exposited by Abba Lerner, the Keynesian policy precepts contained no substitute for the balanced budget. Functional finance required no such rule at all; taxes were to be levied, not for the purpose of financing public outlays, but for the sole purpose of forestalling and preventing inflation.[12] It is indeed interesting to speculate on "what might have been" had the Keynesian economists followed Lerner's lead. The "education" of political leaders, and ultimately of the public, would have been quite different. The principles for policy would have been much simpler, and it is scarcely beyond the realm of plausibility to suggest that the required lessons might have been learned, that a politically viable regime of *responsible* functional finance might have emerged.

But such was not to be. Even the Keynesian economists seemed unwilling to jettison the time-honored notion that the extension and the makeup of the public sector, of governmental outlays, must somehow be related to the willingness of persons to pay for public goods and services, as expressed indirectly through the activities of legislatures in imposing taxes. But how was this tie-in between the two sides of the fiscal account to be reconciled with the basic Keynesian thrust which called for the abandonment of the balanced-budget rule? We have already traced the developments that reflected this tension, from the initial acquiescence in passive imbalance on the presupposition that balance would somehow be achieved over the business cycle, to the

---

12. Abba P. Lerner, "Functional Finance and the Federal Debt," *Social Research* 10 (February 1943): 38–51; and idem, *The Economics of Control* (New York: Macmillan, 1944), pp. 285–322.

more sophisticated notion that a rule of budget balance might be restored, but balance this time at some hypothetically determined level of national income. But we must now look somewhat more closely and carefully at the burden that this new norm places on the political decision maker. He is told by his economists that budget balance at high employment is desirable, and that both outlay and revenue adjustments should be made on the "as if" assumption that the targeted level of income is generated. Once this exercise is completed, he is told, he may then acquiesce in the deficits or surpluses produced by the flow of economic events secure in the knowledge that all is well. This is a deceptively attractive scenario until we recognize that it offers an open-ended invitation to strictly judgmental decisions on what is, in fact, "high-employment" income. Furthermore, it tends to "build in" a presumed trade-off between unemployment and inflation, which may or may not exist.

What is the hypothetical level of income to be chosen for budget balance?—or, if desired, for some overbalance? There may be no uniquely determined level of high-employment income, and economists will surely continue to argue about the degree and extent of genuinely structural unemployment that might be present at any time. Additional definitiveness might be introduced by stipulating that the target income is that which could be generated without inflation. But, if structural unemployment is pervasive, this sort of budgetary norm may suggest balance between revenues and outlays in the face of observed rates of unemployment that are higher than those considered to be politically acceptable. In such a setting, imagine the pressures on the politicians who attempt to justify the absence of a budget deficit, after forty years of the Keynesian teachings.

An additional difficulty arises in the division of responsibility between the fiscal and monetary instruments. With the budget-balance-at-hypothetical-income norm, the tendency may be to place the restrictive burden on the monetary authorities and instruments while adding to this burden by the manipulation of budgetary-fiscal instruments applied to unattainable targets. Consider, for example, the setting in 1975, when we observed *both* unemployment and inflation rates of roughly 8 percent. The balance-at-hypothetical-income norm could have been, and indeed was, used by economists and politicians to justify the budget deficits observed in that year, and to argue for increases in these deficits. The inflation was, in turn, "explained" either by structural elements (administered prices) or by the failures of the monetary authorities to restrain demand. In this latter sense, the monetarists tended to support the Keynesians indirectly because of their emphasis on the purely monetary sources of inflation. This emphasis allows the politicians to expand the budget deficit in putative adherence to the balance-at-high-employment norm, bloating the size of the public sector in the process. To the extent that the responsibility for inflation can be placed on the monetary authorities, the restrictive role for fiscal policy is politically weakened regardless of the budgetary norm that is accepted.[13] Neither the monetarists nor the Keynesians can have it both ways. "Easy money" cannot explain inflation and "fiscal drag" unemployment. Yet this is precisely the explanation mix that was translated directly into policy in 1975, generating the tax-reduction pressures on the one hand and the relatively mixed monetary policy actions on the other.

13. Henry C. Wallich, an economist as well as a member of the Federal Reserve Board, has fully recognized this effect of monetarist prescriptions. He stated: "Increasingly, monetarist prescriptions play a role in political discussions. . . . The elected representatives of the people have discerned the attraction of monetarist doctrine because it plays down the effects of fiscal policy. Deficits can do no major damage so long as the central bank does its job right." Wallich then goes on to suggest that the monetary authorities, "for the same reason, have tended to preserve a degree of faith in Keynesianism." Citations are from Henry C. Wallich, "From Multiplier to Quantity Theory," preliminary mimeographed paper, 23 May 1975.

5. Assessing the Damages

Introduction

We have traced the intrusion of the Keynesian paradigm into our national economic and political environment. We have suggested that the effect is a regime of deficits, inflation, and growing government. But is this necessarily an undesirable outcome? Many economists would claim that the Keynesian legacy embodies an improvement in the quality of economic policy. Deficits, they would argue, are useful and even necessary instruments that may be required for macroeconomic management. Inflation, they would suggest, may be but a small and necessary price to pay for the alleviation of unemployment. Moreover, the growth of government is in some respects not a bane but a blessing, for it improves the potential efficacy of macroeconomic policy. The modern Keynesian must argue that the performance of the economy has been demonstrably improved since the political adoption of the New Economics. Because the effective decision makers have been schooled in the Keynesian principles, the economy should function better, it should be kept within stable bounds, bounds that might be exceeded in the absence of such understanding. Even so late as 1970, Kenneth E. Boulding, himself no doctrinaire Keynesian, declared:

> Our success has come in two fields: one in macro-economics and employment policy. . . . Our success . . . can be visualized very easily if we simply contrast the twenty years after the First World War, in which we had the Great Depression and an international situation which ended in Hitler and the disaster of the Second World War, with the twenty years after the Second World War, in which we had no Great Depression, merely a few little ones, and the United States had the longest period of sustained high employment and growth in its history. . . . Not all of this is due to economics, but some of it is, and even if only a small part of it is, the rate of

return on the investment in economics must be enormous. The investment has really been very small and the returns, if we measure them by the cost of the depressions which we have not had, could easily run into a trillion dollars. On quite reasonable assumptions, therefore, the rate of return on economics has been on the order of tens of thousands of percent in the period since the end of World War II. It is no wonder that we find economists at the top of the salary scale![1]

We cannot, of course, deny that the Keynesian conversion has had substantial effects upon our economic order. We do suggest, however, that these effects may not have been wholly constructive. Keynesianism is not the boon its apologists claim, and, unfortunately, it can scarcely be described as nothing more than a minor nuisance. Sober assessment suggests that, politically, Keynesianism may represent a substantial disease, one that can, over the long run, prove fatal for a functioning democracy. Our purpose in this chapter is to assess the damages, to examine in some detail the costs that Keynesianism, in a politically realistic setting, has imposed and seems likely to impose should it remain dominant in future years.

The Summary Record

Budget deficits, inflation, and an accelerating growth in the relative size of government—these have become characteristic features of the American political economy in the post-Keynesian era. The facts, some of which we cite below, are available for all to see. Disagreement may arise, not over the record itself, but over the relationship between the record and the influence of Keynesian ideas on political decisions. Once again we should emphasize that we do not attribute everything to the Keynesian revolution; and surely there are non-Keynesian forces behind both the persistent inflationary pressures of the postwar era and the accelerating size of the public sector. Our claim is the more modest one that at least some of the record we observe can be "explained" by the impact of the Keynesian influence.

During the 1961–1976 period, there was but one year of federal budget surplus lost among fifteen years of deficit, with a cumulative deficit that ex-

---

1. Kenneth E. Boulding, *Economics as a Science* (New York: McGraw-Hill, 1970), p. 151.

ceeded $230 billion and with a return to budget balance looming nowhere on the horizon. Public spending—at all governmental levels, federal, state, and local—in the United States amounted to 32.8 percent of national income in 1960; this proportion had increased to 43.4 percent by 1975.[2] Moreover, since the 1964 tax reduction, increases in governmental spending have absorbed nearly 50 percent of increases in national income. And during this period of supposedly enlightened economic management, consumer prices increased by almost 90 percent.

This Keynesian period contrasts sharply with the transitional years 1947–1960. During this latter period, there were seven years of deficit and seven years of surplus. Deficits totaled some $31 billion, but these were practically

2. We cannot attribute the increase in state and local government spending over this period directly to the abandonment of the balanced-budget norm, since these units lack powers of money creation and, hence, are effectively constrained by something akin to the old-fashioned fiscal principles. Even here, however, it could be argued that the release of spending proclivities at the federal level may have influenced the whole political attitude toward public spending. Furthermore, much of the observed increase in state-local spending is attributable to federal inducements via matching grants and to federal mandates, legislative, administrative, and judicial.

Along these lines, one might point out that state and local expenditures have actually been increasing relative to federal expenditures since 1960. In 1960, state and local expenditures were 53.5 percent of federal expenditures, but by 1975 this percentage had risen to 62.3 percent. For these data, see the *Economic Report of the President* (Washington: U.S. Government Printing Office, 1976), pp. 249–251. The growth of government, it would appear, has been especially rapid among the lower levels of government.

Such data, however, are exceedingly misleading, for they attribute to state and local governments those expenditures that were financed by grants from the federal government. Such grants totaled $6.9 billion in 1960, and had swollen to $48.3 billion in 1975. Removing such grants from the figures for state and local expenditures changes the interpretation considerably. State and local expenditures are now seen to be 46.1 percent of federal expenditure in 1960, increasing only to 48.8 percent in 1975. Moreover, federal grants customarily are offered on a matching basis, which generally stimulates additional state and local expenditure. This portion of expenditure that is a result of the stimulating input of federal grants should also properly be attributed to the federal government. If it is assumed that each dollar of federal grant stimulates state and local spending by 20¢, state and local spending as a percentage of federal spending was practically stable over the 1960–1975 period, rising only from 43.9 percent to 44.8 percent. The figure of a 20-percent rate of stimulation is consistent with that found in Edward M. Gramlich, "Alternative Federal Policies for Stimulating State and Local Expenditures: A Comparison of Their Effects," *National Tax Journal* 21 (June 1968): 119–129.

matched by the surpluses that totaled $30 billion. This overall budget balance becomes even more striking when it is recalled that the period included the Korean War. Consumer prices increased by 32 percent, an inflationary tendency not found in most previous peacetime periods, but still a low rate when compared with experience since the full-fledged acceptance of Keynesianism. And even this 32-percent figure exaggerates the nature of the inflationary pressures during this transition period, for fully one-half of the total rise in prices occurred during just two years, 1948 and 1951. In other words, the normal rate of price rise during this period was about 1 percent annually.[3]

Budget Deficits, Monetary Institutions, and Inflation

The budget deficits that emerged from the Keynesian revision of the fiscal constitution injected an inflationary bias into the economic order. Empirically, the deficit-inflation nexus is strong and is widely acknowledged in popular discussion. Yet there are economists who would deny that deficits are inflationary. It is important that we make clear our position on this issue.

Monetarists, or at least most of them, would deny that deficit spending in itself is inflationary. They concentrate their fire, and they suggest that inflation results and can result only from an increase in the supply of money relative to the supply of goods. It is increases in the supply of money, not budget deficits, that cause or bring about inflation. We do not deny this monetarist

---

3. That the Truman-Eisenhower years were indeed transitional becomes apparent once it is recalled that such a period previously would have been accompanied by a cumulative budget surplus, with the surplus used to retire public debt. The decade following World War I, 1920–1929, for instance, saw ten consecutive surpluses, with the total surplus exceeding $7.6 billion. This surplus made possible a 30-percent reduction in the national debt. Prices were generally stable, but with a slight downward drift. Prices did fall sharply during the contraction of 1920–1921, but were stable thereafter. Wholesale prices fell by nearly 40 percent between 1920 and 1921, while consumer prices fell by a little over 10 percent. From then on, approximate stability reigned: Wholesale prices fell by slightly less than 3 percent during the remainder of the decade, while consumer prices declined by slightly over 4 percent. Moreover, the share of government in the economy actually declined, falling from 14.7 percent in 1922 (figures for 1920 are not available) to 11.9 percent in 1929.

logic. We do suggest, however, that it is reasonable to describe inflation as one consequence of budget deficits, and hence, indirectly, as a consequence of the Keynesian conversion.[4]

In the customary monetarist framework, the supply of money is treated as an exogenous variable, one determined by the monetary authorities. That is to say, the supply of money is viewed as being inelastic with respect to budget deficits. We do not deny that monetary institutions could be created in which the supply of money was indeed deficit invariant. We do deny, however, that existing monetary institutions are unresponsive to deficits. Simply because one might imagine a setting in which the supply of money is invariant to budget deficits or surpluses does not mean that actual institutions operate in this manner.

As we explore more fully in Chapter 8, existing political and monetary institutions operate to make the supply of money increase in response to budget imbalance. Within our prevailing institutional setting, budget deficits will tend to bring about monetary expansion. Therefore, it is appropriate to claim that budget deficits are inflationary, for such a claim is in fact simply a prediction about the response of our monetary institutions. While it seems entirely reasonable to link inflation more or less directly to budget deficits, this linkage need not imply a rejection of the insights of monetarism in favor of those of fiscalism. On the contrary, it affirms them, but goes further in that it makes a prediction as to the response of contemporary monetary institutions.[5]

---

4. David Laidler and Michael Parkin advance a similar position when they observe: "It is central to modern work on the role of the government budget constraint in the money supply process that an expansionary fiscal policy met by borrowing from the central bank will result in sustained monetary expansion. . . . In the light of this work the question as to whether monetary expansion is a unique 'cause' of inflation seems to us to be one mainly of semantics" ("Inflation: A Survey," *Economic Journal* 85 [December 1975]: 796).

5. The massive cumulative deficit since 1960 has been accompanied by a substantial shortening of the maturity structure of marketable issues of national debt. In 1960, 39.8 percent of such debt was scheduled to mature within one year. By 1975, this figure had expanded to 55 percent. While 12.8 percent of such debt had a maturity date of ten years or longer in 1960, this figure had shrunk to 6.8 percent in 1975. This shortening of the maturity structure reinforced the outright monetization of budget deficits that occurred during this period (Source: *Federal Reserve Bulletin*).

Inflation: Anticipated and Unanticipated

The economic literature on inflation makes much of the distinction between anticipated inflation and unanticipated inflation. This distinction, which is as seductive in its appearance as it is misleading in its message, has had much to do with creating the belief that inflation gives little cause for alarm, a belief that is erroneous in its cognitive foundations.

An unanticipated inflation catches people by surprise, whereas an anticipated inflation catches no one off guard. In the former case, the supply of money expands unexpectedly, driving prices upward. Since people do not know in advance that inflation is imminent and to what extent, they cannot account for it in their long-term contractual arrangements. If inflation is fully anticipated, however, people know in advance that the supply of money will be expanding and that the price level will be rising at a predictable rate. This knowledge enables them to account for the future rise in prices in undertaking their various activities. If price stability should be expected, a person might lend $100 today in exchange for $110 in one year, reflecting a 10-percent annual rate of return on the investment. But suppose that such a contract is made, and the lender finds that the price level rises by 10 percent; the $110 he receives at the end of the year will enable him to buy only what he could have purchased with the initial $100 one year earlier. The unanticipated inflation would have, in this case, reduced his real rate of return to zero. If, however, the potential lender should have anticipated that prices would rise by 10 percent annually, he would have lent only in exchange for the promise of a return of $121 after one year. Only under such an agreement would he expect to get back the initial purchasing power plus a 10-percent return on the investment. As this simple example shows, unanticipated inflation transfers wealth from people who are net monetary creditors to people who are net monetary debtors. With a fully anticipated inflation, by contrast, these transfers could not take place.[6]

A fully anticipated inflation would seem to create some minor irritations—frequent changes in vending machines and more resort to long division—-

6. See the analysis in Reuben A. Kessel and Armen A. Alchian, "The Effects of Inflation," *Journal of Political Economy* 70 (December 1962): 521–537.

but little else. The idealized analytical construction for anticipated inflation allows everyone to know with certainty that prices will rise at some specified annual rate. From this, it follows that the nominal terms of contracts will be adjusted to incorporate the predicted reduction in the real value of the unit of account in terms of which payment is specified. This type of inflationary regime is one of perfect predictability. All persons come to hold the same view as to the future course of prices. There is no uncertainty as to the real value of the unit of account five, ten, or twenty years hence. Economic life is essentially no different from what it would be if the price level were stable.

While the construction of a perfectly anticipated inflation is not descriptive in reality, it does isolate elements that help in explaining behavior. Individuals do learn, and they will try to alter the nominal terms of long-period contracts as they come to feel differently about future inflationary prospects. Continued experience with unanticipated inflation surely leads to *some* anticipation of inflation. But this is not at all the same thing as the anticipation of that rate of inflation which will, in fact, take place. To an important extent, inflation is always, and must be, unanticipated. We do not possess the automatic stability properties of a barter economy, of which the construct of a fully anticipated inflation is one particular form, but possess instead the uncertainties inherent in a truly monetary economy, although alternative monetary institutions may mollify or intensify these uncertainties. Unlike a stylized anticipated inflation, inflation in real life must increase the uncertainty that people hold about the future.

Why Worry about Inflation?

Commonplace in much economic literature is the notion that the dangers of inflation perceived by the general public are grossly exaggerated. Few economists would follow Cagan in describing inflation as a monster, a hydra-headed one at that.[7] Many economists have treated inflation as a comparatively trivial problem, something that is regarded as making rational calculation a bit more difficult, but not much else. The most substantial cost of inflation, according to this literature, is the excess burden that results from the inflation tax on

---

7. See Phillip Cagan, *The Hydra-Headed Monster: The Problem of Inflation in the United States* (Washington: American Enterprise Institute, 1974).

money balances. Under inflation, people hold a smaller stock of real balances than they would hold under price stability or deflation. The loss of utility resulting from this smaller stock is the cost of inflation.[8] The size of this loss will, under plausible circumstances, be quite small, much on the order of the small estimates of the welfare loss from monopoly.

This view seems to us to be in error. Inflation is likely to be far more costly than simple considerations of welfare loss suggest. Several noted economists have recognized the significance of inflation for the long-run character of our economic order. John Maynard Keynes, in whose name the present inflationary thrust is often legitimatized, observed that

> there is no subtler, no surer means of overturning the existing basis of Society than to debauch the currency. The process engages all the hidden forces of economic law on the side of destruction, and does it in a manner which not one man in a million is able to diagnose.[9]

Joseph A. Schumpeter remarked that

> perennial inflationary pressure can play an important part in the eventual conquest of the private-enterprise system by the bureaucracy—the resultant frictions and deadlock being attributed to private enterprise and used as argument for further restrictions and regulation.[10]

The standard economic analysis of inflation rests upon the assumption, as inadmissible as it is conventional, that *inflation does not disturb the underlying institutional framework.*[11] Inflation, it is assumed, sets in motion no forces that operate to change the very character of the economic system. If the possibility of such institutional adaptation is precluded by the choice of analytical framework, it is no wonder that inflation is viewed as insubstan-

---

8. See, for instance, Martin J. Bailey, "The Welfare Cost of Inflationary Finance," *Journal of Political Economy* 64 (April 1956): 93–110; and Alvin L. Marty, "Growth and the Welfare Cost of Inflationary Finance," *Journal of Political Economy* 75 (February 1967): 71–76.

9. John Maynard Keynes, *The Economic Consequences of the Peace* (New York: Harcourt, Brace, 1920), p. 236.

10. Joseph A. Schumpeter, *Capitalism, Socialism, and Democracy,* 3rd ed. (New York: Harper and Row, 1950), p. 424.

11. On this point, see Axel Leijonhufvud's careful, contrary-to-conventional-wisdom analysis of inflation from this institutionalist perspective, "Costs and Consequences of Inflation," manuscript, May 1975.

tial. Once the ability of inflation to modify the institutional framework of the economic order is recognized, inflation does not appear to be quite so benign.

Inflation generates a shift in the relative rates of return that persons can secure from alternative types of activities. The distribution of effort among activities or opportunities will differ as between an inflationary and a noninflationary environment. As inflation sets in, the returns to directly productive activity fall relative to the returns from efforts devoted to securing private gains from successful adjustments to inflation per se.[12] The returns to such activities as developing new drugs, for instance, will decline relative to the returns to such activities as forecasting future price trends and developing accounting techniques that serve to reduce tax liability. The inflation itself is responsible for making the latter sorts of activity profitable ones. In a noninflationary environment, however, such uses would be unnecessary, and the resources could take up alternative employments.

Over and above the direct distortions among earning opportunities that it generates, inflation alters the economy's basic structure of production and disturbs the functioning of markets. Shifts in relative prices are generated which, in turn, alter patterns of resource use. Additionally, inflation injects uncertainty and misinformation into the functioning market structure. Intertemporal planning becomes more difficult, and accounting systems, whose informational value rests primarily on a regime of predictable value of the monetary unit, tend to mislead and to offer distorted signals. As a result, a variety of decisions are made which cannot be self-validating in the long run. Resources will be directed into areas where their continued employment cannot be maintained because the pattern of consumer demand will prove inconsistent with the anticipated pattern of production. Mistakes will come increasingly to plague the decisions of business firms and consumers.[13]

The most substantial dangers from inflation come into view, however, only when we consider the interplay between economic and political forces. As Keynes noted, individual citizens will at best understand the sources and consequences of inflation only imperfectly—first appearances will to some

---

12. See ibid.

13. For an elaboration of these and related issues, see David Meiselman, "More Inflation, More Unemployment," *Tax Review* 37 (January 1976): 1–4.

extent be confounded with ultimate reality. Because of this informational phenomenon, inflation will tend to generate misplaced blame for the economic disorder that results. This makes the inflationary consequences of the Keynesian conversion a serious matter, not a second-order by-product to be dismissed lightly.

For reasons we examine in Chapter 9, inflation, at least as it manifests itself under prevailing monetary institutions, obscures the information signals that citizens receive concerning the sources of decline in their real income. As it *appears to them,* their real income declines not because the government collects more real taxes but because private firms charge higher prices for their products. In consequence, the political pressures emerging from inflation would tend to take the form of suggested direct restraints on the prices charged by business firms, as opposed to widespread public clamor for restraints on "prices" exacted by government.[14]

To see beyond this institutional veil, and to discern that the higher prices of products sold by private business firms are really only a manifestation of higher taxes collected by government, would take considerable effort and skill. The generally undistinguished responses to tests of economic principles that are administered to past economics students cast doubt upon the likelihood that inflation will be viewed simply as an alternative form of taxation. That professional economists would differ sharply among themselves in this matter would seem to cinch the point.

These matters of necessarily incomplete knowledge are compounded by the differential incentives to invest in the attainment of different types of knowledge. Someone who more correctly anticipates the rate of inflation will generally fare better than someone who does not. Relatedly, inflation always presents opportunities for profit through actions designed to exploit the various discrepancies that inflation invariably produces. An individual's own actions, in other words, will directly and immediately influence his net worth, so there is an incentive for him to invest in securing relevant knowledge. But there are no comparable incentives for an individual to invest resources in an

---

14. This point suggests the hypothesis that democracies will impose controls on private producers more rapidly and profusely under inflationary conditions than under conditions of price-level stability. Casual empiricism surely supports this hypothesis, but more sophisticated testing would be helpful.

attempt to understand the cause of inflation. To an individual, there is no economic value in knowing whether the source of his loss in real income is the higher prices charged by business firms or the "counterfeiting" of the government.[15] The citizen cannot trade directly upon knowledge. Only as a majority of citizens come to see inflation in the same way, thereby creating the conditions favorable to a change in governmental policy, will the investment in knowledge come to possess any payoff.

Informationally, then, inflation is likely to be misperceived, at least under present monetary institutions. Individuals are unlikely to see clearly through the institutional veils. Additionally, however, the incentives that exist are such that it is worth very little to persons to discern the correct interpretation of inflation. Unlike the situation with respect to ordinary market choice, there is very little payoff to discerning the truth. These two features reinforce one another to produce a misplaced blame for inflation.

It is the business firms and labor unions that are viewed as being the source of the loss of real income. From this, it follows that controls placed on wages and prices become a popular political response to the frustrations of inflation, especially as the inflation continues and its rate accelerates. The costs of controls, both in terms of economic value and in terms of restrictions on personal liberty, should, therefore, be reckoned as major components of the inclusive costs of inflation.

Inflation, Budget Deficits, and Capital Investment

We do not need to become full-blown Hegelians to entertain the general notion of *zeitgeist*, a "spirit of the times." Such a spirit seems at work in the 1960s and 1970s, and is evidenced by what appears as a generalized erosion in public and private manners, increasingly liberalized attitudes toward sexual activities, a declining vitality of the Puritan work ethic, deterioration in product quality, explosion of the welfare rolls, widespread corruption in both the private and the governmental sector, and, finally, observed increases in

---

15. An anticipation of future rates of inflation can be formed without a correct understanding as to why the inflation is taking place. A long-term historical experience in which prices rise by roughly 10 percent annually will come to inform the nominal terms of trade, regardless of what particular explanation individuals may happen to attribute to the observed inflationary pressures.

the alienation of voters from the political process. We do not, of course, attribute all or even the major share of these to the Keynesian conversion of the public and the politicians. But who can deny that inflation, itself one consequence of that conversion, plays some role in reinforcing several of the observed behavior patterns. Inflation destroys expectations and creates uncertainty; it increases the sense of felt injustice and causes alienation. It prompts behavioral responses that reflect a generalized shortening of time horizons. "Enjoy, enjoy"—the imperative of our time—becomes a rational response in a setting where tomorrow remains insecure and where the plans made yesterday seem to have been made in folly.[16]

As we have noted, inflation in itself introduces and/or reinforces an antibusiness or anticapitalist bias in public attitudes, a bias stemming from the misplaced blame for the observed erosion in the purchasing power of money and the accompanying fall in the value of accumulated monetary claims. This bias may, in its turn, be influential in providing support to political attempts at imposing direct controls, with all the costs that these embody, both in terms of measured economic efficiency and in terms of restrictions on personal liberty. Even if direct controls are not imposed, however, inflation may lend support for less direct measures that discriminate against the business sector, and notably against private investment. In a period of continuing and possibly accelerating inflation, tax changes are likely to be made that adjust, to some extent, the inflation-induced shifts in private, personal liabilities. But political support for comparable adjustments in business or corporate taxation—adjustment for nominal inventory profits, for shifts in values of depreciable assets, and so on—is not likely to emerge as a dominant force. Taxes on business are, therefore, quite likely to become more penalizing to private investment during periods of inflation.

---

16. Wilhelm Röpke recognized this consequence of inflation when he remarked: "Inflation, and the spirit which nourishes it and accepts it, is merely the monetary aspect of the general decay of law and of respect for law. It requires no special astuteness to realize that the vanishing respect for property is very intimately related to the numbing of respect for the integrity of money and its value. In fact, laxity about property and laxity about money are very closely bound up together; in both cases what is firm, durable, earned, secured and designed for continuity gives place to what is fragile, fugitive, fleeting, unsure and ephemeral. And that is not the kind of foundation on which the free society can long remain standing" (*Welfare, Freedom and Inflation* [Tuscaloosa: University of Alabama Press, 1964], p. 70).

Standard accounting conventions have developed largely in a noninflationary environment, and the information that such techniques convey regarding managerial decisions becomes less accurate when inflation erupts.[17] Business profits become overstated, owing both to the presence of phantom inventory profits and to the underdepreciation of plant and equipment. In an inflationary setting, depreciation charges on old assets will be insufficient to allow for adequate replacement. An asset valued at $10 million might, after a decade of inflation, cost $20 million to replace. Since allowable depreciation charges would be limited to $10 million, only one-half of the asset could be replaced without dipping into new supplies of saving. Under FIFO accounting procedures, moreover, "profits" will also be attributed to the replacement of old inventory by new.[18]

The overstatement of business profits is as striking in its size as it is disturbing in its consequences. In nominal terms, post-tax earnings of nonfinancial corporations rose from $38 billion in 1965 to $65 billion in 1974. This 71-percent increase kept pace with inflation during this period, which might convey the impression that real earnings had at least remained constant. The elimination of underdepreciation and phantom inventory profits, however, yields post-tax earnings in 1974 of only $20 billion, nearly a 50-percent decline over this ten-year period. The payment of taxes on what are fictive profits brought about an increase in effective tax rates on corporations of more than 50 percent. A tax rate of 43 percent in 1965 became an effective rate of 69 percent in 1974.[19]

In addition to the consumption of capital that operates indirectly through the ability of inflation to impose taxes on fictive profits, budget deficits may directly retard capital formation as well. The deficit financing of public out-

17. For a general discussion of this point, see William H. Peterson, "The Impact of Inflation on Management Decisions," *Freeman* 25 (July 1975): 399–411.

18. The switch from FIFO to LIFO methods of inventory valuation, which has been taking place in recent years, is one particular attempt to deal with the reduced accuracy of accounting information in an inflationary environment. For a careful examination of this problem, see George Terborgh, *Inflation and Profits* (New York: Machinery and Allied Products Institute, 1974).

19. These figures are reported in Reginald H. Jones, "Tax Changes Can Help Close Capital Gap," *Tax Review* 36 (July 1975): 29–32. See also Norman B. Ture, "Capital Needs, Profits, and Inflation," *Tax Review* 36 (January 1975): 1–4; and C. Lowell Harriss, "Tax Fundamentals for Economic Progress," *Tax Review* 36 (April 1975): 13–16.

lays may "crowd out" private investment, with the predicted result that the rate of capital formation in the economy is significantly reduced over time. The expansion in public borrowing to finance the budget deficit represents an increased demand for loanable funds. While a subsequent rise in interest rates may elicit some increase in the amount of total saving in the economy, the residual amount of saving available to meet the private-sector demands for loanable funds will fall. Utilization of savings by government to finance its deficit will crowd out utilization of savings for private investment.[20]

To illustrate, suppose that, under balanced-budget conditions, $90 billion would be saved, all of which would then be available to private borrowers, to investors. Now suppose that the government runs a $70 billion deficit. Let us say that the resulting rise in the rate of interest would be sufficient to increase private saving by $10 billion, raising total saving to $100 billion. Of this $100 billion, however, government would absorb $70 billion to finance its deficit. This would leave only $30 billion for private investors. The nonmonetized deficit would have reduced the rate of private capital formation by 67 percent below that rate which would have been forthcoming in the absence of the budget deficit. The deficit would, in this example, have crowded out $60 billion of private investment.

The $70 billion borrowed by government could, of course, also be used for capital investment, either directly on public investment projects or indirectly in the form of subsidies to the creation of private capital. To the extent that this happens, a crowding-out effect in the aggregate would be mitigated, although the public-private investment mix would be shifted, raising questions about the comparative productivity of public and private investment. In the modern political climate, however, the funds secured through public borrowing would probably be utilized largely for the financing of budgetary shortfalls, with the lion's share of outlay being made on consumption, directly or indirectly. Transfer payments grew more rapidly than any other component of the federal budget after the early 1960s. The crowding out that would actually occur, then, would be one in which private capital investment was replaced by increased consumption, mostly through transfer payments:

20. This proposition about "crowding out" is surveyed in Keith M. Carlson and Roger W. Spencer, "Crowding Out and Its Critics," *Federal Reserve Bank of St. Louis, Review* 57 (December 1975): 2–17.

Ploughs, generating plants, and fertilizer would be sacrificed for TV dinners purchased by food stamps.

By diverting personal saving from investment to consumption, our capital stock is reduced. The economy will come to be confronted by a "capital shortage." A fiscally induced stimulation of consumption spending would attract resources from higher-order activities to lower-order activities. The structure of production would be modified, and the economy's capital stock might shrink. This process ultimately would reduce rather than increase the volume of consumption services that the economy could provide at a sustained rate. The maintenance of a higher level of consumption over a short period could be accomplished only at the expense of a depreciation of the nation's capital stock. In this scenario, we should be gradually reducing the rate of increase in our capital stock. As a rich nation, we could perhaps sustain this process beyond the limited time horizons of most politicians, but an ultimate reckoning would have to take place.[21]

These issues of capital shortage, and the debate that has taken place over them, serve once again to illustrate the importance of developing an appropriate interpretation of the nature of the economic process. Those who dispute the claim that we are suffering from capital shortage, from a shrinkage of our capital stock, point to the existence of underutilized plant and equipment as evidence in support of their position. The cereal manufacturer who possesses excess capacity, it is suggested, can hardly be said to be suffering from a shortage of capital. What is wrong, rather, is a deficiency of consumption—a surplus of capital, in effect.

The real problem, however, may be a shortage of such complementary capital as wheat, fertilizer, tractors, machine tools, or ovens, all of which, and many more, must cooperate in the production of cereal. A modification of the structure of production may generate some underutilization of capital. And it seems possible that full utilization cannot be restored until the complementary capital is replenished. But such restoration requires additional

---

21. Some comparative figures released by the U.S. Treasury Department are instructive in this respect. During the 1963–1970 period covered by the study, the share of national output that was devoted to additions to the capital stock was considerably less in the United States than in several of the relatively progressive industrialized nations. Our rate of capital investment was 13.6 percent. This rate was 17.4 percent in Canada, 18.2 percent in France, 20 percent in West Germany, and 29 percent in Japan.

saving. The further stimulation of consumption, however, would shrink the capital stock still further, and this shift of the structure of production might make matters even worse. The presence of underutilized capital may be an indication of a shortage of complementary capital, not a surplus of the specific capital itself.[22]

The Bloated Public Sector

Permanent budget deficits, inflation, and an expanding and disproportionately large public sector are all part of a package. They are all attributable, at least in part, to the interventionist bias created by Keynesian economics. Deficits and inflation are related to the growth of government in a reciprocal fashion. Deficits and inflation contribute to the growth of government, while the growth of government itself generates inflationary pressures.

Colin Clark once advanced the thesis that, once government's share in national income exceeds 25 percent, strong inflationary pressures will emerge.[23] Much of the ensuing critical discussion concentrated on Clark's specific mention of 25 percent as the critical limit to the relative size of government. Widely proclaimed refutations of Clark's thesis were reported by Keynesian interventionists as government's share seemed to inch beyond 25 percent without the simultaneous occurrence of strong inflationary pressures. Lost amid these shouts was Clark's general principle that there exists a positive relation between the relative size of government and the strength of inflationary pressures. This thesis of a positive relation between the size of government and

---

22. In this and the immediately preceding paragraphs, we have introduced, all too briefly, elements of the so-called "Austrian theory" of the cycle. We feel that the emphasis on the structural maladjustments that can result from monetary disturbances is an important insight, especially in the political context we have been describing. At the same time, however, we retain essentially a monetarist interpretation of such a phenomenon as the Great Depression, as well as a belief in the usefulness of aggregate demand stimulation under such circumstances. The forces of secondary deflation that operate under rigid wages and prices seem to us to overwhelm those real maladjustments that are those of the primary depression itself. Our position on the relation between the Austrian and monetarist interpretations is quite similar to that found in Gottfried Haberler, *The World Economy, Money, and the Great Depression, 1919–1939* (Washington: American Enterprise Institute, 1976), pp. 21–44.

23. Colin Clark, "Public Finance and Changes in the Value of Money," *Economic Journal* 55 (December 1945): 371–389.

the rate of inflation can be supported from two distinct and complementary perspectives, as we have already indicated.

Harry G. Johnson has supported Clark's thesis by arguing that deficit spending and the resulting inflation have made possible the increasing size of the public sector.[24] We shall examine the general reasons for this in Chapter 7. Johnson suggests that taxpayers would not support the present apparatus of the welfare state if they were taxed directly for all of its activities. Deficit spending and inflationary finance tend to alleviate the intensity of taxpayer resistance, ensuring a relative expansion in the size of public budgets. Inflationary finance becomes a means of securing public acquiescence in larger public budgets.

This knowledge-reducing property of inflation is reinforced in a revenue structure that rests on a progressive tax system. In a narrow sense, inflation is a tax on money balances. In addition, however, inflation brings about increases in the real rates of other taxes. Under a progressive income tax, for instance, tax liability will rise more rapidly than income. For the United States personal income tax, considered in its entirety, estimates prepared from data and rate schedules in the early 1970s suggested that a 10-percent rate of general inflation would generate roughly a 15-percent increase in federal tax collections.

While inflationary finance may stimulate public spending, it is also possible for public spending to create inflation. To the extent that resources utilized by government are less productive than resources utilized by the private sector, a shift toward a larger public sector reduces the overall productivity in the economy. In this sense, an increasing relative size of the public sector, measured by an increasing share of national income represented by public spending, becomes equivalent to a reduction in the overall productivity of resources in the economy.[25] Unless the rate of growth in the supply of money is correspondingly adjusted downward, the public-sector growth must itself be inflationary. Therefore, the growth of public spending may induce inflation at the same time that the inflationary financing of governmental activities lowers taxpayer resistance to further increases in public spending.[26]

---

24. Harry G. Johnson, "Living with Inflation," *Banker* 125 (August 1975): 863–864.

25. See Graham Hutton, "Taxation and Inflation," *Banker* 125 (December 1975): 1493–1499.

26. In recent years, an expanding body of thought, both conceptual and empirical, has

An increasingly disproportionate public sector, quite apart from its inflationary consequences, carries with it the familiar, but always important, implications for individual liberty. The governmental bureaucracy, at least indirectly supported by the biased, if well-intentioned, notions of Keynesian origin, comes to have a momentum and a power of its own. Keynesian norms may suggest, rightly or wrongly, an expansion in *aggregate* public spending. But aggregates are made up of component parts; an expansion in overall budget size is reflected in increases in *particular* spending programs, each one of which will quickly come to develop its own beneficiary constituency, within both the bureaucracy itself and the clientele groups being served. To justify its continued existence, the particular bureaucracy of each spending program must increase the apparent "needs" for the services it supplies. Too often these activities by bureaucrats take the form of increasingly costly intrusions into the lives of ordinary citizens, and especially in their capacities as business decision makers.

International Consequences

Our purpose in this chapter is to offer an assessment of the damages to our economic-political order that may have been produced by the Keynesian conversion. Such an assessment should include some reference to international consequences, although these are, to an extent, mitigated by the simultaneous influences at work in the political structures of almost all of the nations of the West.

Under the traditional gold standard, approximately realized before World

---

been developing in support of the proposition that, at the prevailing margins of choice, resources employed in the public sector are less efficient than resources employed in the private sector. For a sample of this literature, see William A. Niskanen, *Bureaucracy and Representative Government* (Chicago: Aldine, 1971); Thomas E. Borcherding, ed., *Budgets and Bureaucrats* (Durham, N.C.: Duke University Press, 1976); Roger Ahlbrandt, "Efficiency in the Provision of Fire Services," *Public Choice* 16 (Fall 1973): 1–16; David G. Davies, "The Efficiency of Private versus Public Firms: The Case of Australia's Trio Airlines," *Journal of Law and Economics* 14 (April 1971): 144–165; William A. Niskanen, "Bureaucracy and the Interests of Bureaucrats," *Journal of Law and Economics* 18 (December 1975): 617–643; and Richard E. Wagner and Warren E. Weber, "Competition, Monopoly, and the Organization of Government in Metropolitan Areas," *Journal of Law and Economics* 18 (December 1975): 661–684.

War I, a national economy could not operate independently so as to control its domestic price level. If a nation tried to finance budget deficits through in-flationary credit expansion, the international demand for its output would fall. The ensuing gold drainage would reduce the nation's money stock, thereby depressing the nation's price level. Public debt could not be effectively mon-etized under the gold standard. During the period when the United States was on a gold standard, there were annual fluctuations in prices, but changes in one direction tended to be followed by changes in the opposite direction, yielding long-run price stability in the process.[27]

Although much less direct in its impact, the same basic relationship was at work under the less restrictive gold-reserve standard of the years between World War II and the 1970s. Public debt could be monetized in the short run, but the resulting inflation would depress the demand for exports. Balance-of-payments deficits would arise. In the short run, such deficits need have no impact upon the domestic money stock. Eventually, however, deficits would cumulate to the point at which contractions in the domestic money supply would become necessary.[28]

The international monetary system changed dramatically in the 1970s when a regime of floating exchange rates replaced that of fixed rates. This change was hailed, by Keynesian and non-Keynesian economists alike, as a desirable step which would finally allow a single nation to act independently in macro-economic policy. Under free exchange rates, a nation can control its do-mestic money supply unless the government tries to control fluctuations in its own exchange rate, in which case it necessarily relinquishes some of this control.[29] Inflationary policies no longer call forth, either immediately or im-minently, a corrective reduction in the domestic money supply. The exchange rate now adjusts automatically to maintain equilibrium in the balance of pay-

27. For a description and analysis of our movement from a gold standard to a fiduci-ary standard, see Benjamin Klein, "Our New Monetary Standard: The Measurement and Effects of Price Uncertainty, 1880–1973," *Economic Inquiry* 13 (December 1975): 461–484.

28. Haberler suggests that, if there is uniform resistance to deflation, a balance of pay-ments disequilibrium may be resolved through inflation in surplus countries, rather than through deflation in deficit countries. Gottfried Haberler, "The Future of the Interna-tional Monetary System," *Zeitschrift für Nationalökonomie* 34, no. 3–4 (1974): 387–396.

29. For an examination of the relation between the international monetary system and domestic monetary policy, see Harry G. Johnson, *Inflation and the Monetarist Controversy* (Amsterdam: North-Holland, 1972).

ments. Debt can be monetized without the necessity ultimately of reversing the process. This shift in the form of international monetary arrangements, while strengthening the ability of a nation to control its monetary policies,[30] has severed one of the constraints on internal monetary expansion.[31] It does not seem to be entirely a coincidence that deficit spending and inflation have intensified since the shift to free exchange rates. It is possible, of course, that continually falling values of a nation's currency will operate as an effective restraint on domestic monetary expansion. Only time will tell.

Tragedy, Not Triumph

A regime of permanent budget deficits, inflation, and an increasing public-sector share of national income—these seem to us to be the consequences of the application of Keynesian precepts in American democracy. Increasingly, these consequences are coming to be recognized as signals of disease rather than of the robust health that Keynesianism seemed to offer. Graham Hutton has suggested that

> what went wrong was not Keynes' schemes. It was his optimism about politics, politicians, employers and trade unionists. . . . Keynes would have been the foremost to denounce such behaviour as the doom of democracy.[32]

30. David Fand has discussed in some detail the relationship between the shift to floating rates and the prospects for inflation. He argues that the excess reserves produced by the shift tended to be inflationary in the transitional period but that the enhanced control of the national monetary authorities should lead to less inflation over a longer term. In this analysis, Fand neglects the possible increased vulnerability of national monetary authorities to domestic political pressures, a point that we discuss in Chapter 8. See David I. Fand, "World Reserves and World Inflation," *Banca Nazionale del Lavoro Quarterly Review* 115 (December 1975): 3–25.

31. Recognizing this relationship does not necessarily imply the superiority of a fixed exchange-rate system. The choice between a floating and a fixed system rests, finally, on predictions about the operation of domestic decision makers on the one hand and foreign decision makers, in the aggregate, on the other. Floating rates provide protection against exogenous foreign influences on the domestic economy. But, at the same time, they make the economy considerably more vulnerable to unwise manipulation by domestic politicians.

32. Graham Hutton, *What Killed Prosperity in Every State from Ancient Rome to the Present* (Philadelphia: Chilton Book, 1960), p. 96.

The juxtaposition of Keynesian policy prescriptions and political democracy creates an unstable mixture. The economic order seems to become more, rather than less, fragile—coming to resemble a house of cards. A nation's response to such situations is always problematical. It is always easy to assess history from the perspective of hindsight. But the wisdom of hindsight would rarely permit nations and civilizations to deteriorate. Without the benefit of hindsight, we cannot foretell the future. We can, however, try to diagnose our present difficulties, point out possible paths of escape, and explain the dangers that lurk before us.

The ultimate danger in such situations as that which we are coming to confront, one that has been confirmed historically all too frequently, is that we will come to see our salvation as residing in the use of power. Power is always sought to promote the good, of course, never the bad. We are being bombarded with increasing intensity with calls for incomes policies, price and wage controls, national planning, and the like. Each of these aims to achieve its objectives by the imposition of new restrictions on the freedom of individuals. Will our own version of "national socialism" be the ultimate damage wrought by the Keynesian conversion?

PART TWO

What Went Wrong?

6. The Presuppositions of Harvey Road

Introduction

The economic policy results that we have all observed since the mid-1960s, and which seem likely to persist, were not supposed to happen. Once the politicians became enlightened, the New Economics, the heritage of Lord Keynes, was supposed to inform a sequence of rationally based policy decisions, carried forward with due regard to the "public interest." Sustained and sometimes double-digit inflation accompanied by high unemployment was not supposed to emerge; "stagflation" was a bad and impossible dream.

What went wrong? It is, of course, part of the human psyche to turn first to the "evil man" theory for potentially satisfying explanation, modified as appropriate by "stupid man" amendments. And it would, indeed, offer grounds for short-term optimism if the policy disasters we have witnessed could be imputed squarely to either the deliberate machinations of corrupt politicians or the folly of the unwise. We fear, however, that such an imputation would simply be escapism. The election of neither more honest nor more enlightened politicians will resolve our difficulties.

The outcomes we are witnessing are produced by the juxtaposition of the Keynesian amendment of our fiscal constitution and our form of democratic political process. The applicability of any set of policy rules or precepts is not invariant over alternative decision-making institutions. An idealized set of policy prescriptions may be formulated for a truly benevolent despotism. But this set may be far distant from the ideal prescriptions for the complex "game" of democratic politics, a game that involves the participation of citizens as voters who are simultaneously taxpayers and public-service beneficiaries, the activities of professional politicians whose electoral successes depend on pleasing these voters, the struggles of the sometimes fragile coalitions reflected in organized or unorganized political parties, and, finally, the machinations of bureaucrats who are employed by government but who tend, indirectly, to control the details of government operation.

The Presuppositions of Harvey Road

There is little mystery about Keynes' own assumptions concerning the politics of economic policy. Personally, he was an elitist, and his idealized world embodied policy decisions being made by a small and enlightened group of wise people. But these "presuppositions of Harvey Road,"[1] as they are called by his biographer, extended beyond idealization. Economic policy decisions must be made in the real world, and these Keynesian presuppositions also impinged on reality. Keynes not only envisaged government by an enlightened and small elite as his ideal; he also assumed that, at base, this model described government as it actually was observed to operate.

These political presuppositions of Keynes, as were and are those of many of his professional colleagues before and since, were probably influenced by a mixture of positive and normative elements. Keynes held important positions in the British government, and his ideas exerted notable influence on policy, especially during World War I. He probably exaggerated his own role in policy decisions. Furthermore, as so many who knew him personally have remarked, Keynes was an extremely persuasive man in argument, and confidence in his own ability to convince others may have led him to discount

---

1. "We have seen that he [Keynes] was strongly imbued with what I have called the presuppositions of Harvey Road. One of these presuppositions may perhaps be summarized in the idea that the government of Britain was and could continue to be in the hands of an intellectual aristocracy using the method of persuasion" (R. F. Harrod, *The Life of John Maynard Keynes* [London: Macmillan, 1951], pp. 192–193). Harvey Road was the location of the Keynes family residence in Cambridge.

As Smithies put it: "Keynes hoped for a world where monetary and fiscal policy, carried out by *wise men* in authority, could ensure conditions of prosperity, equity, freedom, and possibly peace.... He thus hoped that his economic ideas could be put into practice outside the arena of partisan politics, but failed to realize that his own efforts tended to make this impossible" (Italics supplied; Arthur Smithies, "Reflections on the Work and Influence of John Maynard Keynes," *Quarterly Journal of Economics* 65 [November 1951]: 493–494).

the potential importance of genuinely differing attitudes that might emerge in a collective decision process. His biographer, R. F. Harrod, suggests this when he questions the applicability of the presuppositions in a setting different from that assumed by Keynes.

> If, owing to the needs of planning, the functions of government became very far-reaching and multifarious, would it be possible for the intellectual aristocracy to remain in essential control? Keynes tended till the end to think of the really important decisions being reached by a small group of intelligent people, like the group that fashioned the Bretton Woods plan. But would not a democratic government having a wide multiplicity of duties tend to get out of control and act in a way of which the intelligent would not approve? This is another dilemma—how to reconcile the functioning of a planning and interfering democracy with the requirement that in the last resort the best considered judgment should prevail. It may be that the presuppositions of Harvey Road were so much of a second nature to Keynes that he did not give this dilemma the full consideration which it deserves.[2]

Normatively, Keynes was no democrat, in any modern descriptive meaning of this term. To the extent that Keynes might have predicted interferences with rational policy to emerge from the sometimes grubby institutions of electoral and party politics, he would have been quite willing to jettison such institutions, regardless of their history and of their traditional role. Perhaps it is best simply to say that Keynes was not particularly concerned about institutions, as such. His emphasis was on results and not on rules or institutions through which such results might be reached. And if institutional barriers to what he considered rational policy planning should have worried him, Keynes would have been ready to set up a "national planning board" run by a committee of the wise.[3]

2. Ibid., p. 193.

3. This is clearly indicated by Keynes' statement in the foreword to the German edition of his *General Theory:* "Nonetheless, the theory of output as a whole, which is what the following book purports to provide, is much more easily adopted to the conditions of a totalitarian state, than is the theory of production and distribution of a given output produced under the conditions of free competition and a large measure of laissez-faire" (Quoted and translated in George Garvey, "Keynes and the Economic Activists of Pre-Hitler Germany," *Journal of Political Economy* 83 [April 1975]: 403).

It is important to recognize explicitly what Keynes' political presuppositions were because the policy implications of his "general theory" were developed within this framework. We observe, however, that, for the United States in particular, these policy precepts have been advanced as appropriate for a political framework that scarcely resembles that postulated by Keynes.[4] If the form of government is relevant for economic policy, we must at least question this unchallenged extension.

The preliminary response of the orthodox economist would be to suggest that his role does not require that he pay attention to the institutional means through which his ideas might or might not be accepted and implemented. A widespread and often implicit conviction to this effect has prevented even the most elementary recognition of the possible linkage between politics and policy. The orthodox economist, whether Keynesian or non-Keynesian, whether macroeconomist or microeconomist, has remained essentially uninterested in the political setting within which economic ideas may or may not be translated into reality. To explain this long-observed and continuing insularity of the economic theorist from politics, from public choice, would require a separate treatise, replete with methodological argument. For our purposes, we take this insularity as fact. Knut Wicksell noted, as early as 1896, that economists had almost all proceeded on something resembling the Keynesian presuppositions, on the notion that their role was one of proffering advice to a benevolent despot.[5]

And this frame of mind has continued to the present, despite the observed presence of democratic choice-making processes. Herschel Grossman, in reviewing the contributions of James Tobin to macroeconomics, has described clearly this failure of economists to recognize that macroeconomic policy emerges through democratic politics, not from the board room of a com-

---

4. Paul A. Samuelson suggested the opposite, while affirming our thesis in the process, when he argued that "America, rather than Britain, was the natural place where the Keynesian model applied: the United States was largely a closed, continental economy with an undervalued dollar that gave ample scope for autonomous macroeconomic policies . . ." (Samuelson, "Hansen as a Creative Theorist," *Quarterly Journal of Economics* 90 [February 1976]: 26). By ignoring the institutions through which policy emerges, Samuelson, like Keynes, seems to be accepting the presuppositions of Harvey Road.

5. Knut Wicksell, *Finanztheoretische Untersuchungen* (Jena: Gustav Fischer, 1896). Translated as "A New Principle of Just Taxation," in Richard A. Musgrave and Alan T. Peacock, eds., *Classics in the Theory of Public Finance* (London: Macmillan, 1958), pp. 72–118.

mittee of the wise. While particular references were to Tobin, Grossman was speaking of economists in general when he noted:

> Tobin presumes that the historical record of monetary and fiscal policy in-
> volves a series of avoidable mistakes, rather than the predictable conse-
> quences of personal preferences and capabilities working through the ex-
> isting constitutional process by which policy is formulated. Specifically,
> Tobin shows no interest in analysis of either the economically motivated
> behavior of private individuals in the political process or the behavior of
> the government agents who make and administer policy.[6]

The Economic Environment of the "General Theory"

Why should political institutions influence economic policy? Why should policy norms that are found to be applicable under one structure for collective
decision making be inappropriate or inapplicable in an alternative structure?
These questions might be disposed of readily, indeed in summary fashion, if
the choice among separate policy options were always sharp and clear, if precepts of rationality suggested a dominant policy strategy. It is in this respect
that the economic environment within which the Keynesian theory was developed becomes relevant for understanding the neglect, by both Keynes and
the Keynesians, of the political framework. In the setting of the early and
most elementary Keynesian model, no rational government, regardless of organization, could fail to carry forward the policy norms that seem to emerge
so clearly from the "general theory"; this being so, the political framework
for decision could be treated as largely irrelevant.

Let us summarize this elementary model. The aggregate supply curve runs
horizontally to some point that is labeled "full-employment income," beyond
which the curve turns sharply upward. The economy in underemployment
equilibrium is then depicted by the intersection of the aggregate demand
curve with the aggregate supply curve along the horizontal portion of the
latter. The policy implication becomes evident; aggregate demand should be
increased. There is no other way to increase employment and output. But,

---

6. Herschel I. Grossman, "Tobin on Macroeconomics: A Review Article," *Journal of Political Economy* 83 (August 1975): 845–846.

from another set of diagrams or equations, we can also see that the economy is caught in a liquidity trap. Interest rates are at a floor, and additional money creation alone will merely add to hoards; private spending will not be affected. Additional government spending becomes the natural policy consequence, with deficit creation indirectly implied.

We are not interested here in examining either the logical coherence or the empirical validity of the description of the national economy that is embodied in this most basic of Keynesian models. Our emphasis is on the attitudes of those who accepted such a model of economic reality as the ground upon which to construct policy prescriptions. In the depression-stagnant economy depicted here, the creation of a deficit in the government's budget seems clearly to be dictated by rational policy norms, requiring only the acknowledgment that full employment and expanded real output are appropriate objectives. Why would any person, placed in a responsible decision-making position, raise objections to the policy prescribed if he understood the argument? Consider the elected member of a legislative assembly, a congressman or a senator. Deficit creation involves either a reduction in taxes and/or an increase in public spending. Both of these actions, taken independently, are desired by citizens-constituents. There are no offsetting costs to balance against the benefits; more of everything may be secured. There seems here to be no possible conflict between "politics" on the one hand and the true "public interest" on the other. Good politics seems good policy, and opposition can be traced to the presence of outdated and inappropriate fiscal rules.

If the elementary Keynesian diagnosis-description of underemployment equilibrium is accepted, and, furthermore, if this is considered to be a possible permanent state of the economy in the absence of corrective governmental action, the economist will tend to stress the clear and distinct benefits that stem from the indicated policy action, and he will tend to be blind to attempts at rational refutation. He will, in addition, find it nearly impossible to imagine that the institutional barriers of practical politics can permanently frustrate the clearly defined vision that the revolutionary Keynesian model offers him. If we place ourselves in the stance of the early Keynesian enthusiasts, we should perhaps not be surprised at their neglect of political structure.

These enthusiasts did not critically question the logical coherence or the empirical validity of the model, nor did they examine carefully the applicability of the policy norms in other situations, despite the claims of having developed a general theory. The interest was concentrated on restoring prosperity; the prevention of inflation was not considered to be even so much as a potential problem. How could we have expected the early enthusiasts of the revolution in ideas to foresee the political impracticality of applying the Keynesian policy tools in such a converse setting?

Strings Can Be Pulled

The continued stance of those who called themselves "Keynesian" after the end of World War II should not be so sympathetically interpreted. Keynes died in 1946, and we have no means of judging how his own attitude might have been shifted by his observation of events. After 1946, our strictures apply to those who considered themselves to be the preachers of the Keynesian gospel, the textbook writers, the economic journalists, the governmental counselers.

The facts were soon clear in the immediate postwar years. The American economy was not settling down to a permanent underemployment equilibrium. Inflation, not unemployment, seemed to be the threat to prosperity. Aggregate demand was excessive, not deficient, and the Keynesian tools were, at best, awkward in their application. Under the political presuppositions of Harvey Road, these tools were symmetrical in application. Budget surpluses should have been created to mop up the excessive demand.

Instead, in early 1948, taxes were reduced in the United States. Should not this action have given early pause to those Keynesian economists who had hitherto paid almost no heed to the workings of democratic process? It should have been evident that the fiscal policy precepts emerging from the simple Keynesian analysis were one-sided in their practical application. The creation of surpluses would have been recognized as politically different in kind from the creation of budget deficits. In retrospect, it seems likely that the political biases of the whole Keynesian edifice would have been acknowledged in the early postwar period, had it not been for the simultaneous "rediscovery" that money matters. This allowed the responsibility for demand restriction to be shifted temporarily from fiscal policy to monetary policy instruments, which were allegedly adjusted under a set of institutions that fit the Harvey Road presuppositions.

We should recall that, in its early and elementary form, the Keynesian policy model embodied a total disregard of money and of monetary policy. In underemployment equilibrium, money creation alone was alleged to be ineffective in stimulating aggregate demand. The government's budget became the central policy instrument, and, by implication, it was the only instrument required to maintain national economic prosperity. Under the presumption that fiscal policy application was fully symmetrical, monetary policy could be neglected whether stimulation or restriction in aggregate demand was needed. Monetary policy could, therefore, be relegated to a subsidiary role of facilitating credit markets, and it might be directed mainly toward keeping interest rates at or near the liquidity floor as a means of encouraging investment. But experience under this policy, in both the United States and Great Britain, soon suggested that, unless genuinely draconian fiscal measures were to be undertaken as offsets, inflation was not likely to be controlled. Monetary policy was quickly reincorporated into the sophisticated Keynesian's set of instruments, and the efficacy of monetary restriction on reducing aggregate demand was acknowledged.

Indirectly, the Keynesian economists who modified their norms to allow for the use of monetary policy instruments when demand restriction seemed to be needed were acknowledging the political asymmetry of the whole Keynesian structure. They did not, however, do so consciously, and they continued to talk in terms of some idealized application of both fiscal and monetary policy tools. In one of his best-known policy statements, Paul Samuelson called for a policy mix of "easy money" and "tight budgets," designed to ensure a high rate of investment and capital formation while holding down consumption spending to avoid inflationary pressures.[7] In this idealized set-

---

7. In this 1963 statement, Samuelson noted that this policy package had been "advocated for many years by such liberal economists as James Tobin, E. C. Brown, R. A. Musgrave and me." See Paul A. Samuelson, "Fiscal and Financial Policies for Growth," in *Proceedings—A Symposium of Economic Growth* (Washington: American Bankers Association, 1963), pp. 78–100. Reprinted in *The Collected Scientific Papers of Paul A. Samuelson*, vol. 2, ed. Joseph Stiglitz (Cambridge, Mass.: MIT Press, 1966), pp. 1387–1403; citation from p. 1402.

As early as 1955, Samuelson had explicitly posed this policy mix, but without strong advocacy. See his "The New Look in Tax and Fiscal Policy," Joint Committee on the Economic Report, 84th Congress, 1st Session, *Federal Tax Policy for Economic Growth and Sta-*

ting, budget surpluses, which could be financed by tax increases, well might be required in order to allow for the expansion in the demand for investment goods generated by the low interest rates. Samuelson's position was widely accepted and discussed by economists, as if the postwar fiscal experience had not happened, as if the "presuppositions of Harvey Road," or their American counterparts, remained descriptive of political reality.

Little or no sophisticated insight should have been required to suggest that, at best, the fiscal and monetary policy instruments would tend to be applied nonsymmetrically in political democracy. Budgets would rarely, if ever, be observed to be overbalanced as a result of purposeful efforts at demand restriction. "Easy budgets" promised to be the order of the day, and especially during periods of recession, regardless of magnitude. On the other hand, if demand was to be restricted at all during periods of threatened inflation, this task would fall to the monetary authorities, who did seem to possess some nominal independence from the political process, at least in the sense of direct constituency pressures. The best policy package that might have been predicted to emerge was clearly one of "easy budgets and tight money," just the reverse of the Samuelson norm.[8]

The Great Phillips Trade-off

The incorporation of monetary policy instruments for the purpose of restricting spending might have occurred even if the form of the aggregate supply function assumed in the early Keynesian models had been proved to be an accurate representation of the underlying economic reality. If the aggregate demand curve cuts the aggregate supply curve to the right of the full-

---

bility, November 1955, pp. 229–234. Reprinted in *Papers of Paul A. Samuelson,* vol. 2, pp. 1325–1330.

For evidence to the effect that modern economists continue to accept the Keynesian political presuppositions, we may look at a 1975 Brookings Institution analysis of capital needs, in which it is argued that capital shortage concerns can be alleviated if the federal government follows a budget-surplus, easy-money policy. See Barry Bosworth, James S. Duesenberry, and Andrew S. Carron, *Capital Needs in the Seventies* (Washington: Brookings Institution, 1975).

8. The political pressures generating this result were discussed in James M. Buchanan, "Easy Budgets and Tight Money," *Lloyds Bank Review* 64 (April 1962): 17–30.

employment kink or corner, inflation control rather than employment stimulation becomes an objective, even in the most naive of Keynesian models. The postwar record soon revealed, however, that this simple functional form was far from descriptive. There was no horizontal portion of an aggregate supply curve, and models based on the presumption that such a portion exists were likely to produce biased results. There were no kinks; increases in aggregate demand did not exert an effect wholly, or even largely, on employment and output up to some magic point labeled "full employment," and only thereafter commenced to exert upward pressures on prices in the economy. If an aggregate supply relationship was to be used at all, empirical reality seemed to dictate that this be shown diagrammatically as a curve that sloped upward throughout its range. This suggested the presence of a continuing trade-off between the two acknowledged objectives for national economic policy, between employment and price stability.

The converse of this relationship, that between the rate of unemployment and the rate of price inflation, became the central topic for discussion among macroeconomists for the better part of two decades. The "Phillips curve," which depicts this alleged trade-off, found its way into the textbooks in elementary economics, replacing earlier Keynesian supply functions.[9] We shall discuss some of this Phillips-curve analysis in more detail in Chapter 11. Our purpose here is limited to questions concerning how the recognition of such a trade-off might have modified economists' political presuppositions and, in turn, how the political framework itself might have become more significant for policy outcomes in the presence of Phillips-curve trade-offs.

The relationship dramatically modified the setting for macroeconomic policy choice. Even during periods of recession, when aggregate demand might have seemed to be deficient by some standards, policies designed to increase total spending in the economy were not costless. Additional output and employment, acknowledged as desirable, could be attained only at the expense of some inflation, equally acknowledged as undesirable. There simply was no

---

9. The influential paper was A. W. Phillips, "The Relation between Unemployment and the Rate of Change in Money Wage Rates in the United Kingdom, 1951–1957," *Economica* 25 (November 1958): 283–299. The relationship had been noted much earlier and was statistically estimated by Irving Fisher in 1926. For a discussion of the history, see Donald F. Gordon, "A Neo-Classical Theory of Keynesian Unemployment," *Economic Inquiry* 12 (December 1974): 434ff especially.

horizontal portion of some aggregate supply curve where employment might be increased without inflation, where increased employment was, in this sense, "costless" to achieve. The Phillips curve suggested that a trade-off between mutually desirable but mutually conflicting objectives was likely to be present, regardless of the state of the national economy.

No single set of policy actions dominated all others; rational, intelligent, and fully informed persons might differ as to the relative weights to be assigned to alternative objectives. Whether inflation should be stimulated as a means of securing more employment, or some unemployment should be accepted as the price for holding inflation within bounds, was a question that could be answered only in terms of basic social values, about which persons might differ. Even under the Keynesian presuppositions about policy making, even with governmental economic policy decisions in the hands of a few wise people, who could now predict their actions? No longer did the policy precepts emerge with clarity from the economists' analytical model of the world.

The Phillips curve was alleged to depict the set of possible outcomes; the choice among these possible positions was to be made on the basis of the community's preferred rate of trade-off between the components. Economists diagrammed all of this by introducing a set of community or social indifference curves, and they could then indicate some "optimal" policy choice as that which allowed the community to attain its highest level of utility.[10] This construct was then utilized to interpret aspects of political reality; the shift in economic policy between the Eisenhower and Kennedy administrations was almost universally interpreted as a shift in the relative weights assigned to the inflation control and the employment objectives.

It should have been clear that the presence of a Phillips-curve trade-off between unemployment and inflation would make the institutions of decision making, the politics of policy, more important rather than less so. Despite this, economists continued to ignore this element in their diagnoses and prescriptions. Even for a group of enlightened people, decisions on relative weights could scarcely remain wholly immune from political feedbacks.

10. This formulation of "optimal" policy choice was initiated in Paul A. Samuelson and Robert M. Solow, "Analytical Aspects of Anti-Inflation Policy," *American Economic Review, Papers and Proceedings* 50 (May 1960): 177–194.

Until and unless the public, acting upon and through their elected political representatives, generally could be depended on to understand and to acquiesce in the weights assigned, tension would be set up between the decision makers and the community at large. The New Economics, which now was Keynes amended by the Phillips-curve trade-off, was not so simple as before. Consider the potential for policy conflict when a public opinion and political attitude partially reflecting the norms of the earlier simplistic Keynesian model were imposed on a set of policy decisions emerging from the allegedly more sophisticated Phillips-curve analytics. Unemployment might be observed to exist; full-employment income, defined by some presumed Keynesian kink in an aggregate supply curve, was not being generated. The simple Keynesian precepts might then have called for increases in total spending, for increased budget deficits, without much if any recognition of the dangers of inflation. By contrast, the economic decision makers, whoever they might be, might recognize the existence of a Phillips trade-off, but how could they fail to remain unaffected by the prevailing public-political attitudes? Could we not predict an inflationary bias in the Phillips-curve world, even under the presuppositions of Harvey Road?

Post-Keynes, Post-Phillips

Perhaps we are lucky that the inflation-unemployment relationship discussed so widely under the Phillips-curve rubric (which has not yet disappeared from the elementary textbooks) was, like the simple Keynesian model that preceded it, doomed to be disavowed and discredited under the weight both of logical analysis and of accumulating empirical evidence. In a short-run context, additional employment and output may be stimulated by increases in total spending, accompanied by some unanticipated inflation in prices. If, however, explicit policy measures designed to add to total spending are continued over a sequence of periods, inflation will come to be anticipated, and inflationary expectations will be built into the whole structure of negotiated contracts. From this point in time, the generation of inflation that has been predicted will do nothing toward stimulating employment and output. If, in fact, it could be realized, a fully predicted and steady rate of inflation will ensure the same overall level of employment that would have been ensured with a zero rate; in this setting, there is no Phillips-curve trade-off. To secure a further short-run increase in employment, the rate of increase in total spending and the rate of inflation must be accelerated, and the acceleration itself must be unanticipated. Once the community finds itself saddled with inflationary expectations, however, attempts to reduce the rate of inflation will themselves have the same results as reductions in aggregate demand in a more stable setting. Unemployment may be generated by attempts to do nothing more than hold the rate of inflation within tolerable limits.

For long-run policy planning, the evidence as well as the logic suggests that there is, in effect, no sustainable trade-off between unemployment and inflation. There exists neither the Keynesian kink nor the modified Phillips slope. Aggregate demand increases cannot permanently stimulate employment. The rate of employment can be influenced by such things as minimum-wage legislation and the monopolistic practices of trade unions, but not by changes in aggregate demand.[11]

Our concern here is not with evaluating critically the evidence that has modified economists' attitudes, which has caused many economists who earlier called themselves "Keynesians" to become increasingly skeptical of the selfsame policy norms they espoused in the 1960s. Our concern is with the effect that this change in attitudes and analysis might have had on economists' presuppositions about the political process and on the feedback influences that this process itself exerts on economic policy.

We are lucky in that the creeping inflationary bias introduced by the Phillips-curve paradigm was exposed earlier than might have been the case if the underlying empirical realities had been as depicted. The Keynesian tool kit is bare in the world of the 1970s and 1980s. And this is independent of the structure of political decision making. Even if wise persons of Whitehall or Washington, as envisaged by Keynes and the Keynesians, should be empowered to make macroeconomic policy without influence from the grubby world of everyday politics, they could scarcely attain satisfactorily full employment simultaneously with an acceptable rate of inflation. To the extent that such persons were honest as well as wise, they would have to turn to non-Keynesian tools, to those that might attack the structure of labor markets, to those that might open up opportunities for investment and for employment.

---

11. For an explanation, see Milton Friedman, "The Role of Monetary Policy," *American Economic Review* 58 (March 1968): 1–17.

The contrast between what an enlightened elite would impose as economic policy and the actions that we, in fact, observe was never so great as in the post-Keynes, post-Phillips era of the 1970s. As noted earlier, there could have been little or no such contrast in the deep depression of the 1930s, if only the politicians had learned their Keynesian lessons. And, during the Phillips-curve years, disagreements might have emerged only over the relative weights assigned to conflicting objectives. In the post-Phillips setting, however, we observe massive budget deficits, high rates of inflation, and high levels of unemployment. Those who accept the Keynesian political presuppositions in the normative sense, those who feel that a few wise people should be empowered to direct the lives of the rest of us, must now base their argument on the allegation that things would indeed be better if only politics did not intervene.

Reform through National Economic Planning

Perhaps this, in itself, represents progress in understanding. At least those who blame the workings of modern democratic processes for the sorry state of economic policy are indirectly acknowledging that the institutional structure does exert its influence. The distance is shortened between this acknowledgment and possible suggestion for institutional reform. But two separate and divergent routes to reform may be taken, one which we may label "democratic," the other clearly as "nondemocratic." Unfortunately, those who tend to be most critical of democratic politics tend to support structural changes that will, if implemented, remove economic policy decisions from democratic controls. These reformers seek to force upon us something like the institutions postulated under the presuppositions of Harvey Road. If we have not been, and are not yet, ruled by an elite and self-chosen small group, these critics say, so much the worse for us. Such a ruling group "should" be established, empowered with authority, and divorced from the feedbacks of electoral politics. "National economic planning," done through some "National Economic Council" or "National Planning Board," could, presumably, save the day. Not surprisingly, given the acknowledged loss of faith in the Keynesian gospel, articulate demands for "planning" surfaced with some fanfare in 1975, after a quiescence of thirty years. These demands took the form of discussion surrounding a proposed legislative program introduced by Senators Humphrey and Javits, a program supported by a few prominent economists.[12]

How could a group of planners genuinely divorced from politics, an "economic supreme court," resolve the American dilemma of stagflation? As suggested above, they could accomplish little by even the most skillful use of the basic Keynesian tools. How could more careful manipulation of the federal budget or of monetary policy secure both full employment and a return to price-level stability after the orgies of the 1965–1976 period? Inflation could, of course, be brought within bounds; price-level stability can be accomplished. But how could this be done, save at the expense of unacceptably high levels of unemployment, higher even than those experienced in 1975?

An incomes policy, a euphemism for wage and price controls, could be imposed, only with more firmness and strictness than in 1971. Decisions about prices and wages would be orchestrated by a committee of experts; such decisions would no longer be left to agreement among free individuals over their terms of contract. Such controls have an ancient history, dating back at least to the Code of Hammurabi in the eighteenth century B.C. While such controls historically have invariably failed, they have created much damage in the process. The efforts to evade and avoid the controls come about through a diminution in the "socially" productive activities of individuals, so levels of economic well-being consequently decline.

Alternatively, a planning board, intent on achieving the dual objectives of full employment and price-level stability, could work on the structure of national labor markets. Such a board would find it necessary to intervene directly in the economic order, as it exists within politically imposed boundaries and constraints. An "economic supreme court" could, for example,

---

12. The Balanced Growth and Economic Planning Act of 1975 included the proposed establishment of a complex set of both executive and congressional offices of national economic planning, along with complex coordination procedures. This proposed legislation was subsequently replaced by the Full Employment and Balanced Growth Act of 1976, commonly discussed as the Humphrey-Hawkins bill, which also embodies the creation of an advisory committee along with complex procedures for coordination. Over and beyond this, the proposed act mandated an unemployment target of 3 percent, to be attained within four years. For a generalized critique of the concept of national economic planning, see L. Chickering, ed., *The Politics of Planning* (San Francisco: Institute for Contemporary Studies, 1976).

declare minimum-wage regulation to be contrary to some implicit "economic constitution." In so doing, a sizeable increase in employment, and notably among members of teenaged minority groups, could be secured. But this and other comparable steps which would possibly improve the working of labor markets seem clearly out of bounds through normal legislative processes. Does it seem likely that Congress would consciously delegate such powers of economic policy making to any appointed officials, whether these be designated as members of a national planning board or anything else?

In contrast to nondemocratic approaches to reform, a quite distinct avenue for reform lies in the prospect that the democratic political processes themselves can be improved. Is it not more consistent with American political tradition that the institutions of decision making impose upon politicians constraints that will ensure against the excesses that have emerged from the widespread political acceptance of the Keynesian policy norms? The prudent person acts wisely when he imposes behavioral rules upon himself, rules that may bind his actions over a series of unpredictable future steps. Is it impossible to expect that prudent members of democratic assemblies of governance could do likewise? Should we not look for genuine institutional reform within the structure of democratic decision making rather than for changes that replace this structure?

We shall discuss possibilities and prospects for democratic reform in some detail in Chapter 12. Before we can do so, however, we must first understand the problem that we confront. We must first analyze carefully the reasons democratic decision making, as it exists in the United States, has produced the economic policy results that we observe in the 1970s. We must drop all pretense that economic policy decisions are, or should be, made by a small and well-informed group of people seeking the "public interest." We must escape the blinders imposed on us by all presuppositions akin to those of Harvey Road. We must look at the application and acceptance of Keynesian economics in a political setting where democracy is reality, where policy decisions are made by professional politicians who respond to demands, both of the public and of the bureaucracy itself.

7. Keynesian Economics in Democratic Politics

Introduction

Whether they like it or not, those who seek to understand and ultimately to influence the political economy must become political economists. Analysis that is divorced from institutional reality is, at best, interesting intellectual exercise. And policy principles based on such analysis may be applied perversely to the world that is, a world that may not be at all like the one postulated by the theorists. Serious and possibly irreversible damage may be done to the institutions of the political economy by the teaching of irrelevant principles to generations of potential decision makers. Has the teaching of Keynesian economics had this effect? The question is at least worthy of consideration.

We might all agree that something has gone wrong. The record of deficits, inflation, and growing government is available for observation. We must try to understand why this has happened before we can begin to seek improvement. Our central thesis is that the results we see can be traced directly to the conversion of political decision makers, and the public at large, to the Keynesian theory of economic policy. At a preliminary and common-sense level of discussion, the effects of Keynesian economics on the *democratic* politics of budgetary choice seem simple and straightforward, whether treated in terms of plausible behavioral hypotheses or of observable political reality. Elected politicians enjoy spending public monies on projects that yield some demonstrable benefits to their constituents. They do not enjoy imposing taxes on these same constituents. The pre-Keynesian norm of budget balance served to constrain spending proclivities so as to keep governmental outlays roughly within the revenue limits generated by taxes. The Keynesian destruction of this norm, without an adequate replacement, effectively removed the constraint. Predictably, politicians responded by increasing spending more than tax revenues, by creating budget deficits as a normal course of events. They did not live up to the apparent Keynesian precepts; they did not match the deficits of recession with the surpluses of boom. The simple logic of Keynesian fiscal policy has demonstrably failed in its institutional application to democratic politics.

At a more fundamental level of discussion, however, many issues arise. Even when we acknowledge that the Keynesian presuppositions about a ruling elite are inapplicable to the American scene, we still must ask: Why do our elected politicians behave in the way that the record indicates? Public-choice theory tells us that they do so largely because they expect voters to support them when they behave in such a fashion. But this merely shifts our attention backward to the behavior of voters. Why do voters support politicians who behave irresponsibly in the fiscal sense? What is there about the widespread public acceptance of Keynesian economics that generates the fiscal experience we have witnessed since the early 1960s? There is a paradox of sorts here. A regime of continuous and mounting deficits, with subsequent inflation, along with a bloated public sector, can scarcely be judged beneficial to anyone. Yet why does the working or ordinary democratic process seemingly produce such a regime? Where is the institutional breakdown?

Budgetary Management in an Unstable Economy

Keynesian policy is centered on the use of the government's budget as the primary instrument for ensuring the maintenance of high employment and output. The implementation of Keynesian policy, therefore, required both the destruction of former principles of balanced public budgets and the replacement of those by principles that permitted the imbalance necessary for Keynesian budgetary manipulation. But politicians, and the public generally, were not urged, by Keynes or by the Keynesians, to introduce deficit spending without a supporting logical argument. There was more to the Keynesian revolution than mere destruction of the balanced-budget principle as a permanent feature of the fiscal constitution. This destruction itself was a reasoned result of a modified paradigm of the working of an economy. And, in the larger sense, this is really what "Keynesian" is all about, as we have already noted in Chapter 3. The allocative bias toward a larger public sector and the monetary bias toward inflation are both aspects of, and to an extent are contained within, a more comprehensive political bias of Keynesian economics, namely, an "interventionist bias," which stems directly from the shift in paradigm.[1]

In an inherently unstable economy, government intervention becomes practically a moral imperative. And there is no argument for allowing for a time period between some initially observed departures and the onset of policy action. "Fine tuning" becomes the policy ideal.[2] The notion of an unstable economy whose performance could be improved through the manipulation of public budgets produced a general principle that budgets *need not* be in balance. There would be years of deficit and there would be years of surplus, with these deficits and surpluses being necessary for macroeconomic management. A stable relation between revenues and expenditures, say a relatively constant rate of surplus, would actually indicate a failure on the part of government to carry out its managerial duties.

As we noted in our earlier discussion of the Keynesian political framework, the budgetary policies were to be applied symmetrically. In the Harvey Road political setting, it might even be said that Keynesian economics did not destroy the principle of a balanced budget, but merely lengthened the time period over which it applied. The Keynesian paradigm, in other words, would not be viewed as essentially changing the fiscal constitution within which economic policy is conducted. But what happens when we make non-Keynesian assumptions about politics?

---

1. See Karl Brunner, "Knowledge, Values, and the Choice of Economic Organization," *Kyklos* 23, no. 3 (1970): 558–580, for an examination of the impact of paradigms, which provide the framework for interpreting experiences, upon particular elements of public policy. See W. H. Hutt, *A Rehabilitation of Say's Law* (Athens: Ohio University Press, 1974), for an interpretative survey of Say's Equality.

2. A direct corollary of the view that aggregative shifts are not self-correcting is the notion, even if this is implicit, that such shifts cannot themselves be the results of distorting elements in market structure. Applied to employment, this suggests a tendency to attribute all shifts downward in observed rates of employment to fluctuations in aggregate demand. In such a policy setting, government intervention to correct for increased unemployment that is, in fact, caused by labor market dislocation and structural rigidities acts to cement the latter into quasipermanence and to make ultimate correction more difficult.

Taxing, Spending, and Political Competition

The political process within which the Keynesian norms are to be applied bears little or no resemblance to that which was implicit in Keynes' basic analysis. The economy is not controlled by the sages of Harvey Road, but by politicians engaged in a continuing competition for office. The political decision structure is entirely different from that which was envisaged by Keynes himself, and it is out of this starkly different political setting that the Keynesian norms have been applied with destructive results. Political decisions in the United States are made by elected politicians, who respond to the desires of voters and the ensconced bureaucracy. There is no center of power where an enlightened few can effectively isolate themselves from constituency pressures. Furthermore, since World War II, the national economy has never been appropriately described as being in depression of the sort idealized in the elementary Keynesian models. Throughout the three decades of postwar experience, increases in aggregate demand have always been accompanied by increases in price levels, by inflation.

In a democracy, the pressures placed upon politicians to survive competition from aspirants to their office bear certain resemblances to the pressures placed upon private entrepreneurs. Private firms compete among themselves in numerous, complex ways to secure the patronage of customers. Politicians similarly compete among themselves for the support of the electorate, and they do this by offering and promising policies and programs which they hope will get them elected or reelected. A politician in a democratic society, in other words, can be viewed as proposing and attempting to enact a combination of expenditure programs and financing schemes that will secure him the support of a majority of the electorate. These similarities suggest that political competition is not wholly unlike market competition.

There are also obvious and important differences between market and political competition. Market competition is continuous; at each instance of purchase, a buyer is able to select among alternative, competing sellers. Political competition is intermittent; a decision is binding for a fixed period, usually two, four, or six years. Market competition allows several competitors to survive simultaneously; the capture by one seller of a majority of the market does not deny the ability of the minority to choose its preferred supplier. By contrast, political competition has an all-or-none feature; the capture of a majority of the market gives the entire market to a single supplier. In market competition, the buyer can be reasonably certain as to just what it is he will receive from his act of purchase. This is not true with political competition, for there the buyer is, in a sense, purchasing the services of an agent, but it is an agent whom he cannot bind in matters of specific compliance, and to whom he is forced to grant wide latitude in the use of discretionary judgment. Politicians are simply not held liable for their promises and pledges in the same manner that private sellers are. Moreover, the necessity for a politician to attain cooperation from a majority of politicians produces a situation in which the meaning of a vote for a politician is less clear than that of a vote for a private firm. For these reasons, as well as for several others, political competition differs in important respects from market competition, even where there is also a fair degree of similarity.[3]

The properties of political competition and the characteristics of the budgetary policy that emerge may be examined in several ways. Indeed, the public-choice literature now possesses a variety of analytical models designed to explore and explain the properties of alternative institutional frameworks for political competition.[4] A government can provide a single service, or it can provide a combination of services. It can finance its budget by a variety of tax forms, either singly or in combination, and, additionally, it can subject any particular tax to a variety of rate schedules and exemption rules. Furthermore, preferences for public services can differ as among individual citizens; particular features of the political system can vary; and budget imbalance can be permitted.

Changes in any of these particular features will normally change the budgetary outcomes that emerge. Changes in tax institutions, for instance, will normally change the tax shares and tax prices assigned to different persons. This, in turn, will alter individual responses to particular budgetary patterns. The number of services provided may also matter. With a single service, it is

---

3. For a more complete examination of similarities and differences, see James M. Buchanan, "Individual Choice in Voting and the Market," *Journal of Political Economy* 62 (August 1954): 334–343. Reprinted in James M. Buchanan, *Fiscal Theory and Political Economy* (Chapel Hill: University of North Carolina Press, 1960), 90–104.

4. For a recent survey of the literature on the properties of political competition, see William H. Riker and Peter C. Ordeshook, *An Introduction to Positive Political Theory* (Englewood Cliffs, N.J.: Prentice-Hall, 1973).

fruitful to conceptualize budgetary outcomes in a plurality electoral system as conforming to the preferences of the median voter. With multiple services, however, the conceptualization is not necessarily so simple, for a trading of votes may take place among persons over issues.

The essential features of democratic budgetary choice may be illustrated quite simply. This may be done by considering the gains and losses to politicians of supporting alternative-sized budgets. Suppose for now that a balanced-budget constraint exists. We can start with a budget of zero, and then take account of the gains and losses in terms of constituent support from expansions in the size of the budget. Under the assumption that public output enters positively into the utility functions of citizens, the expenditure by itself will secure support for the politician. The taxes, however, will reduce the disposable income of citizens, thereby affecting them negatively and reducing support for the politician. In a plurality electoral system, for given preferences and fixed tax institutions, the budget will be expanded so long as a majority would prefer the public service to the private goods they would have to sacrifice via taxation.[5]

A detailed description of the various analytical possibilities concerning the character of political competition in a democratic society would require a survey of a quite complex literature.[6] For our purposes in this book, however, the central notions we have just described are sufficient. What this line of analysis suggests is that the consideration by politicians of the gains and losses in terms of constituent support of alternative taxing and spending programs shapes the budgetary outcomes that emerge within a democratic system of political competition. The size and composition of public budgets in such a system of competitive democracy, in other words, can be viewed as a product of the translated preferences of a subset of politicians' constituents and the constitutional-institutional rules that constrain the political system.[7]

---

5. Anthony Downs, *An Economic Theory of Democracy* (New York: Harper and Row, 1957), pp. 51–74, suggested that the size of the budget in a democracy can be viewed as the outcome of a process in which politicians continue to expand the budget so long as the marginal vote gain from public expenditure exceeds the marginal vote loss from the taxation required to finance the expenditure.

6. See Riker and Ordeshook for such a survey.

7. To remain in office, the politician need not meet the demands of all constituents. Instead, he need satisfy only a required subset, usually a majority. Because majority coa-

Unbalanced Budgets, Democratic Politics, and Keynesian Biases

With a balanced-budget rule, any proposal for expenditure must be coupled with a proposal for taxation. The elimination of this rule altered the institutional constraints within which democratic politics operated. Two subtly interrelated biases were introduced: a bias toward larger government and a bias toward inflation. Before examining the foundations of the inflationary bias, it may be useful to examine the relationship between these two biases.

The allocative bias stems from the proposition that, if individuals are allowed to finance publicly provided goods and services through borrowing rather than through taxation, they will tend to "purchase" more publicly provided goods and services than standard efficiency criteria would dictate.[8] The inflationary bias stems from the proposition that, for any given level of public goods and services, for any size of the budget, individuals will tend to borrow rather than to undergo current taxation, at least to an extent beyond the financing mix that would be ideally dictated by either classical or Keynesian criteria. The first bias entails the hypothesis that, because of government borrowing, government spending will be excessive; the second bias entails the hypothesis that, regardless of spending levels, government *borrowing* will be excessive.[9] The public-choice analytical framework makes it possible to see how taxation and debt finance exert differing effects on observed political outcomes. In considering the nature of the pressures of political competition

---

litions shift as among different policy issues, the behavior of the politician who seeks to maintain majority support need not reflect properties of rationality normally attributable to an individual who chooses among private alternatives. This feature of democratic politics has been exhaustively discussed by social scientists since Kenneth Arrow formally proved what he called the "impossibility theorem" in 1951. See Kenneth J. Arrow, *Social Choice and Individual Values* (New York: Wiley, 1951).

8. It should be noted that our analysis does not imply that government borrowing is never justified. Under certain conditions, resort to borrowing may be required for efficient fiscal decisions. Our analysis does suggest that, unless constraints are introduced to ensure that borrowing is limited to such conditions, the opportunity for borrowing will bring about an expansion in the size of the public sector.

9. If, in fact, there should be no effective difference between government debt issue and taxation, essentially the Ricardian view, which we examine in more detail in Chapter 9, neither of these biases would be of import. The first would not exist at all, while the second would be meaningless.

in a revised, Keynesian constitutional setting, we shall consider, in turn, budget surpluses and budget deficits.

Budget surpluses and democratic politics

The creation of (or an increase in) a budget surplus requires an increase in real rates of tax, a decrease in real rates of public spending, or some combination of the two. In any event, creating or increasing budget surpluses will impose direct and immediate costs on some or all of the citizens in the community. If taxes are increased, some persons in the community will have their disposable incomes reduced. If public spending is reduced, some current beneficiaries of public services will be harmed. In terms of direct consequences, a policy of budget surpluses will create losers among the citizenry, but no gainers.

Indirectly, there may be some general acceptance of the notion that the prevention of inflation is a desirable objective for national economic policy.[10] It could be argued that citizens should be able to see beyond the direct consequences of budget surpluses. They should understand that a budget surplus might be required to prevent inflation, and that this would be beneficial. The dissipation of what would otherwise be a surplus through public spending or tax cuts, therefore, would not be costless, for it would destroy those benefits that would result from the control of inflation.

These direct and indirect consequences impact quite differently, however, on the choice calculus of typical citizens. The direct consequences of the surplus take the form of reductions in *presently enjoyed* consumption. If taxes

10. Our analysis here is limited to the demonstration that the symmetry in the creation of budget surpluses and deficits required for efficacy in the operation of a Keynesian-oriented fiscal policy will not emerge in political democracy in the absence of constitutional constraints. We shall not, at this point, discuss the political problems that arise in the creation of budget surpluses when the purpose is that of reducing the size of the public debt outstanding, independently of fiscal policy considerations. Many of the same difficulties in trading off short-term costs for long-term gains would, of course, arise. And perhaps the strongest support for the basic hypothesis that the Keynesian conversion has effectively changed the fiscal constitution lies in the dramatic difference between the pre-Keynesian and the post-Keynesian record of debt retirement. Despite the short-term costs, budget surpluses were created, and public debt was retired, in all postemergency periods prior to World War II in the United States.

are raised, the consumption of private services is reduced; if expenditures are reduced, the consumption of public services is reduced. In either case, the policy of budget surplus requires citizens to sacrifice services that they are presently consuming.

The indirect consequences, on the other hand, are of an altogether different nature psychologically. The benefit side of the surplus policy is never experienced, but rather must be *creatively imagined*, taking the form of the hypothetical or imagined gains from avoiding what would otherwise be an inflationary history. This is a gain that, by its very nature, can never be experienced, but can be only imagined as it is created in the mind of the individual citizen.[11]

A variety of evidence suggests that these choice alternatives are dimensionally quite distinct. Moreover, the sensed benefits from the surplus would be diminished by the severity of the information requirements that confound the citizen's efforts constructively to imagine the benefits that would result from a surplus. The choice is not at all a simple matter of choosing whether or not to bear $100 more in taxes this year in exchange for $120 of benefits in two years, and then somehow to compare the two, historically distinct moments in being. The imagining process requires an additional step. The person must form some judgment of just how he, personally, will fare from the surplus; he must reduce his presumption of the aggregative impact of the surplus to a personal level. As such future gains become more remote and less subject to personal control, however, there is strong evidence suggesting that such future circumstances tend to be neglected, with "out of sight, out of mind" being the common-sense statement of this principle.[12]

---

11. This point about the categorical difference between present and future has been a theme of many of the writings of G. L. S. Shackle. A terse statement of this theme appears in his *Epistemics and Economics* (Cambridge: Cambridge University Press, 1972), p. 245: "We cannot have experience of actuality at two distinct 'moments.' The moment of actuality, the moment in being, 'the present,' is *solitary*. Extended time, beyond 'the moment,' appears in this light as a figment, a product of thought" (Shackle's italics).

12. And even to the extent that citizens do creatively imagine such alternative, conjectural futures, democratic budgetary processes may produce a different form of bias against the surplus. To the extent that budgetary institutions permit fragmented appropriations, for instance, a public-choice analogue to the prisoners' dilemma will tend to operate to dissipate revenues that might produce a budget surplus. Suppose, for instance, that a potential $10 billion budget surplus is prevented from arising because of the pre-

In sum, budget surpluses would seem to have weaker survival prospects in a political democracy than in a social order controlled by "wise men." Budget surpluses may emerge in a democratic political system, but there are institutional biases against them. A person may oppose the creation of a budget surplus for any one or any combination of the following reasons:

1. He may be among those whose taxes will be directly increased, or among those whose benefits from publicly supplied goods and services will be reduced.
2. He may be among those who consider their own economic position (as workers, as investors, and as owners of assets) to be vulnerable to downward shifts in aggregate demand.
3. And he may be among those who anticipate the prospect of making economic gains from inflation.

For any one or any combination of these three reasons, a person may object to demand-decreasing budgetary adjustments. In offset to this, there remains only some generally hazy notion that price-level stability is preferred to inflation, along with some sort of understanding that this objective is supposed to be related to his own direct tax and benefit streams. Viewed in this light, there really should be no difficulty in understanding why we have never observed the explicit creation of budget surpluses during the post-Keynesian years.

BUDGET DEFICITS AND DEMOCRATIC POLITICS

In a democratic society, there would be no political obstacles to budget deficits in an economy with genuine Keynesian unemployment. Budget deficits make it possible to spend without taxing. Whether the deficit is created (or increased) through reduced taxes or increased expenditures, and the partic-

---

sentation of ten separate spending proposals of $1 billion each, as opposed to the presentation of a single expenditure proposal of $10 billion. In the first case, although each participant may recognize that he would be better off if none of the spending proposals carry, institutions that allow separate, fragmented budgetary consideration may operate to create a result that is mutually undesirable. For an analysis of this possibility, see James M. Buchanan and Gordon Tullock, *The Calculus of Consent* (Ann Arbor: University of Michigan Press, 1962), Ch. 10 especially.

ular forms of each, will, of course, determine the distribution of gains among citizens. The central point of importance, however, is that, directly, there are only gainers from such deficits, no losers. In the true Keynesian economic setting, of course, this is as it should be.

The problem with deficit finance is not that it would be supported in a Keynesian economic setting, but that it would also be supported even if the economy were distinctly non-Keynesian. Once the constitutional requirement of budget balance is removed, there are pressures for budget deficits, even in wholly inappropriate, non-Keynesian economic circumstances. If we assume that the money supply is at all elastic in response to budget deficits, a proposition that we support in Chapter 8, deficits must be inflationary in a non-Keynesian economy. The direct effects of budget deficits are sensed only in terms of personal gains. The creation or increase of a deficit involves a reduction in real tax rates, an increase in real rates of public spending, or some combination of the two. In any event, there are direct and immediate gainers, and no losers, regardless of whether the economy suffers from Keynesian unemployment or is blessed with full employment.

In a non-Keynesian economy, deficits will indirectly create losers through the consequences of inflation. These indirect consequences, however, are dimensionally different from the direct effects, just as they were with respect to budget surpluses. The direct consequences of deficit creation take the form of increased consumption of currently enjoyed services. These would be privately provided services if the deficit involves a tax reduction, and would be publicly provided services if the deficit involves an increase in public output.

The indirect consequences, by contrast, relate not to present experience, but to future, conjectured experience. The benefit of deficit finance resides in the increase in currently enjoyed services, whereas the cost resides in the inflationary impact upon the future, in a creatively imagined reduction in well-being at some future date. The analysis of these indirect consequences is essentially the same as that of the indirect consequences of budget surpluses, so there is little to be gained from repeating the analysis in detail. It suffices to say that the act of creatively imagining the future is compounded by the twin factors of remoteness and the absence of personal control.

Democratic societies will tend to resort to an excessive use of debt finance when they have permitted Keynesianism to revise their fiscal constitutions. Deficit finance will generate political support, even in a non-Keynesian economy, among those persons for whom either of the following two conditions holds:

1. persons who are among those whose real taxes will be reduced or among those who expect to experience an increased flow of benefits from government, including receipt of direct monetary transfers; and
2. persons who are among those who consider their own economic positions (as employees, as investors, as owners of real assets, or bureaucrats) likely to be improved as a result of the increase in aggregate demand.

These direct supporting consequences may even be supplemented by a general, but unnecessary, notion that increased real output and employment are worthy objectives for national economic policy coupled with some idea that these may be achieved by the creation of deficits. In opposition of deficits, there is only some future sensed anticipation of the benefits resulting from living in the absence of the inflation, with its various consequences, that would otherwise have taken place.

The post-Keynesian record in fiscal policy is not difficult to understand. The removal of the balanced-budget principle or constitutional rule generated an asymmetry in the conduct of budgetary policy in competitive democracy. Deficits will be created, but to a greater extent than justified by the Keynesian principles; surpluses will sometimes result, but they will result less frequently than required by the strict Keynesian prescriptions. When plausible assumptions are made about the institutions of decision making in political democracy, the effect is to create biases against the use of budgetary adjustments that are aimed at the prevention and control of inflation, and biases toward budgetary adjustments that are aimed at stimulating employment.

Deficit Finance and Public-Sector Bias

This bias toward deficits produces, in turn, a bias toward growth in the provision of services and transfers through government. Deficit financing creates signals for taxpayers that public services have become relatively cheaper. Because of these signals, voters will demand a shift in the composition of real output toward publicly provided services (including transfers). The "true" opportunity costs of public goods relative to private goods will not, of course, be modified by the use of the budget for purposes of stabilization. To the extent that voters, and their elected legislators, can recognize these "true" cost ratios, no public-spending bias need be introduced. It does not, however, seem at all plausible to suggest that voters can dispel the illusion of a relative price change between public and private goods.[13]

Consider the following highly simplified example. In the full-employment equilibrium assumed to have been in existence before an unanticipated shortfall in aggregate demand, the government provided *one* unit of a public good, and financed this with a tax of $1. The restoration of full employment requires a monetary-fiscal response of 10¢. Suppose now that the response takes the form of reducing tax rates. Taxes fall so that only 90¢ is collected while $1 continues to be spent. The tax price per unit of public output is only 90 percent of its former level. At any tax-price elasticity greater than zero, equilibrium in the "market" for the public good can be restored only by some increase in quantity *beyond one unit,* with the precise magnitude of the increase being dependent on the value of the elasticity coefficient. So long as individuals concentrate attention on the value of public goods, defined in the numeraire, there will be a clear bias toward expanding the size of the public sector in real terms, despite the presumed absence of any underlying shift in tastes.[14]

For this effect to be operative, individuals must confront tax institutions in which marginal tax price moves in the same way as average tax price. This requirement is met with most of the familiar tax instruments; proportional and progressive income taxation, sales taxation, and property taxation all possess this attribute. Tax reductions are normally discussed, and implemented, through reductions in *rates* of tax applied to the defined base. So long as a deficit-facilitated tax reduction takes this form, the terms of trade between public goods and private goods will seem to shift in favor of the former.

The institutionally generated illusion, and the public-spending bias that

13. Budget surpluses, of course, would have the reverse relative price change. We consider only the consequences of deficit because democratic political institutions produce a bias toward deficits, not toward surpluses.

14. The model summarized here is essentially equivalent to the one analyzed more fully in James M. Buchanan, "Fiscal Policy and Fiscal Preference," *Public Choice* 2 (Spring 1967): 1–10. Reprinted in James M. Buchanan and Robert D. Tollison, eds., *Theory of Public Choice* (Ann Arbor: University of Michigan Press, 1972), pp. 76–84.

results from it, can be dispelled if marginal tax prices are somehow held constant while tax collections are reduced inframarginally. If a deficit-facilitated tax cut could take this latter form, there would be no substitution effect brought into play; individuals would continue to confront the same public-goods–private-goods trade-off, *at the margin,* before and after the shift in fiscal policy. It is difficult, however, to construct permanent institutional arrangements that will meet this marginal tax-price criterion. For temporary tax cuts, a pure rebate scheme accomplishes the purpose. Such action does not modify tax rates *ex ante,* and, hence, marginal tax prices. A pure rebate scheme that is not anticipated offers an allocatively neutral scheme of injecting new currency into an economy during a temporary lapse into a pure Keynesian setting. If, however, the spending shortfall is expected to be permanent, and to require continuing injections, rebates will come to violate allocational neutrality for familiar reasons. As soon as persons come to anticipate the *ex post* rebates in making their budgetary decisions *ex ante,* they will act as if marginal tax prices are reduced. To forestall the bias toward public-sector spending in this permanent setting, some other institutional means of maintaining constancy in marginal tax prices would have to be developed.

The one-sided application of Keynesian policy remedies, which emerges from a democratic political setting, may itself create instability in the process. It has increasingly come to be realized that inflation may not generate employment. In fact, inflation may attract resources into employments that cannot be maintained without further inflation.[15] The combined inflationary and interventionist bias of the Keynesian paradigm, therefore, may inject instability into a non-Keynesian economy. In this fashion, the application of Keynesian prescriptions may create a self-fulfilling prophecy, a possibility that

---

15. See Friedrich A. Hayek, *Prices and Production,* 2d ed. (London: Routledge and Kegan Paul, 1935), for an early though neglected explanation of this theme. It should perhaps be noted that Hayek developed his analysis in terms of an excessive attraction of resources into the production of capital goods. This resulted from monetary expansion which drove the market rate of interest below the real rate. In these days of massive public spending, however, the story is more complex, for the objects of the increased public spending also generate an excessive attraction of resources.

we consider in Chapter 11. Keynesianism, in other words, may have changed the fiscal constitution in political democracy, and with destructive consequences.[16]

16. Milton Friedman has offered much the same assessment of the political impact of Keynesianism: Keynesian policy norms "are part of economic mythology, not the demonstrated conclusions of economic analysis or quantitative studies. *Yet they have wielded immense influence in securing widespread public backing for far-reaching governmental interference in economic life*" (Italics supplied; Milton Friedman, *Capitalism and Freedom* [Chicago: University of Chicago Press, 1962], p. 84).

8. Money-Financed Deficits and Political Democracy

Introduction

In Chapter 7, we examined the predicted effects of the Keynesian conversion on political outcomes within a policy-instrument framework that is itself basically Keynesian. We explicitly confined attention to the creation of budget deficits and surpluses for the purpose of macroeconomic management. We paid only secondary attention to the means of financing deficits or the means of disposing of surpluses, save for trying to make explicit the most familiar Keynesian presumption that deficits are financed by the sale of government bonds to citizens and nonbanking firms within the economy, and that budget surpluses are disposed of by the retirement of debt held by these same groups.

As we noted, there has been continuing confusion generated by a stubborn failure to distinguish carefully between genuine public borrowing and money creation. We have tried to make this distinction explicit. The logical next step in the analysis is to consider money creation. Central or national governments, directly or indirectly, possess three means of financing outlays: taxation, borrowing, money issue. The first is eliminated by definition if a deficit is to be created. We have examined the borrowing alternative. We now must look at pure money issue.

Initially, we shall do so within the same basic policy setting utilized in Chapter 7. That is, we shall assume that fiscal adjustments—budgetary management, the creation of deficits or surpluses—provide the primary instruments for the implementation of macroeconomic policy. The analytical model of the preceding chapter is modified only by the assumption concerning the means of financing deficits and of disposing of surpluses. Genuine government borrowing and debt retirement are now replaced by pure money issue and pure money destruction. Furthermore, these offer the only means of changing the supply of money. For purposes of analysis, we initially make the artificial assumption that there exists no independently operative monetary authority. That is to say, the Federal Reserve Board would become, in this model, merely a part of the Treasury.

In the second part of this chapter, we shall shift from the basic Keynesian policy setting toward a monetarist one. This alternative is developed in three sections. In the first, we shall examine the political biases of Keynesian-oriented fiscal policy that is operative alongside a fully effective and wholly independent monetary authority. We shall see what results might be predicted to emerge when we juxtapose a biased fiscal policy and an unbiased monetary policy, where the decision makers for the latter are assumed to be truly benevolent and genuinely wise persons. In the second of the three sections, we drop the independence and wisdom assumptions and replace these by the plausible hypothesis that monetary authorities are, like elected politicians, subjected to both direct and indirect political pressures, and that they need not be all-knowing. Finally, in the last section of the chapter, we shall make an attempt to apply the analyses of both Chapters 7 and 8 to an institutional setting that seems roughly descriptive of the American economy in the late 1970s and early 1980s.

Budget Deficits Financed by Money Creation

In many respects, the economic effects of money-financed deficits are simpler to analyze than those of debt-financed deficits. Since no interest is paid on money, and since a dollar is a dollar regardless of date of issue, money creation, unlike debt creation, involves no future tax liabilities. There is no proposition fully analogous to the Ricardian equivalence theorem which attempts to deny the macroeconomic efficacy of debt-financed deficits.[1] The

---

1. In an economic environment where an increase in the supply of money causes prices to rise, some rational expectations models may produce something akin to the Ricardian proposition. In this case, there would be no output-employment effects of money-financed deficits, even in the short run. Money-financed deficit creation would, in this model, be a form of current taxation, with no real effects on disposable income and no substitution effect as between public and private goods. These models seem, however, to be even more bizarre in the informational requirements they place on individuals

basic Keynesian proposition should command wider acceptance. The creation of a budget deficit, along with its financing by pure money issue, will increase the rate of spending in the economy.

Assume initially that the government's budget is balanced, with outlays and revenues equal. From this position, current rates of taxation are reduced so as to reduce revenues, with governmental outlays remaining unchanged. Suppose that resulting deficit is financed solely by money creation. In the Keynesian paradigm, the disposable incomes of persons in the economy increase. This will, in turn, increase the rate of spending on goods and services in the private sector. To the extent that output and employment are below, or potentially below, "full-employment" levels, the increase in spending will motivate an increase in real output and in employment. To the extent that the aggregate supply function is upward sloping (the economy is characterized by a Phillips-curve trade-off), the increase in the rate of spending will also drive prices higher. If the aggregate supply function is vertical (the economy is in a post-Phillips setting), the effects will be to increase the rate of monetary spending without any increase in real output and employment.

In any of these economic settings, the substitution effect emphasized earlier with debt-financed deficits will come into play. Persons will sense that publicly supplied goods and services are relatively lower in "price" than they were before the fiscal policy shift. This remains true whether the shift involves a simple tax-rate reduction, an increase in budgetary outlays, or some combination of both. By the first law of economics, persons will "demand" a larger quantity of the goods and services that have been reduced in price. This demand will take the form of pressures brought to bear on elected politicians for expansions in the levels of budgetary outlay. There will be the same public-sector bias from the acceptance of Keynesian economics as that which we previously discussed in the debt-financing case.[2]

---

than is the comparable Ricardian model. For instance, they require that the expectations of economic agents are the same as those implied by the solution of the economic model in which they are assumed to exist. Ah, but if only all economists could agree upon a single model! For an exposition by a true believer, of which there are several, see Robert J. Barro, "Rational Expectations and the Role of Monetary Policy," *Journal of Monetary Economics* 2 (January 1976): 1–32.

2. One means of eliminating the public-sector bias might involve the institutionalization of Musgrave's analytical separation of the budget into branches. A constitutional rule

This public-sector bias is, of course, derivative from the basic prediction that fiscal policy shifts will themselves be biased toward demand-increasing rather than demand-decreasing actions, and for the reasons discussed in Chapter 7. The fundamental bias toward inflation will be, if anything, more severe in a regime in which budgetary unbalance is residually adjusted through changes in the money supply than one in which this is adjusted through changes in public debt. History provides perhaps the best corroboration of this hypothesis. Governments have been more severely restricted in their powers of money creation than in their abilities to borrow. Economic history abounds with evidence to the effect that, when allowed a choice, governments tend to inflate their currencies rather than to impose taxation. A begrudging, and possibly subconscious, recognition of this long-standing principle may have been partially responsible for the early Keynesian emphasis on debt financing rather than on the simpler and more persuasive money financing of deficits, within the confines of the elementary Keynesian settings.

Here, as at many other points in this book, we feel ourselves to be triturating the obvious. To say that there will be an inflationary bias when governments are allowed to create deficits and to finance these with currency is very elementary common sense. It is only some of our colleagues in economics who might deny this principle. They might ask: "Why should governments take action that will cause inflation? Why should citizens support politicians whose actions cause inflation?" To the extent that money-financed deficits generate price increases, the fiscal policy shift can be analyzed as the mere substitution of one form of tax for another. If we remain strictly at the level of analysis that does not consider institutional forms of extracting resources from citizens to be relevant for decisions, there need be no predict-

---

might require that the allocation budget be kept strictly in balance, while a separate stabilization branch might be empowered to issue new money and distribute it directly to citizens (by helicopter drop or otherwise) on the one hand, and to levy taxes and to destroy the proceeds on the other. The effective operation of such a set of institutions could eliminate the public-sector bias resulting from the "price" effect discussed. The inflationary bias would not, however, be eliminated under such a regime, and, if anything, the political pressures on an independently organized stabilization branch might be even more severe than those present under a consolidated budget. For the original discussion of the analytical basis of the three-branch budget, see R. A. Musgrave, *The Theory of Public Finance* (New York: McGraw-Hill, 1959).

able effects of this change in taxation, save for those which might emerge from changes in the distribution of tax shares among persons and groups.

Among all forms of extracting resources, however, inflation is perhaps the most indirect, and it is the one that probably requires the highest degree of sophisticated understanding on the part of the individual. Even to analyze inflation as a form of taxation seems open to serious question when our ultimate purpose is that of understanding human behavior. Governments do not present inflation as a form of tax, as a balancing item in published budget projections or reviews. Governments instead make efforts to attribute the causes of inflation to nongovernmental entities and events—profit-hungry capitalist firms and greedy trade unions, foreign cartels, bad harvest, and the like. If the effects of money issue, in terms of behavioral reactions, should be, in fact, equivalent to those of a tax, there would seem to be no point in all such activities of politicians. Something a bit closer to reality is approximated by the popular references to inflation as the "hidden tax." But the reality itself is much more simple. Elected politicians approve programs of public spending; they impose taxes. If they are not required to balance projected spending with revenues, they will not, because the voting public does not hold them directly responsible for the inflation that their actions necessarily produce.

As noted, however, the institutional model discussed in this part of the chapter is artificial. For purposes of symmetry with the treatment of debt-financed deficits in Chapter 7, it has seemed advisable to look at the consequences of money-financed deficits on the presumption that an independent monetary authority does not exist. If this were at all descriptive of reality, the relationship between deficit creation and inflation might be much more readily perceived by citizens, who might then hold elected politicians to account for irresponsible actions. But it is precisely the existence of a quasi-independent monetary authority, nominally empowered to control the supply of money, that increases the "noise" in the whole system of relationships between fiscal action and changes in the values of the basic macroeconomic variables. This point should become clear in the later discussions in this chapter.

Benevolent and Independent Monetary Authority

In our discussion of debt-financed deficits in Chapter 7, we assumed, more or less implicitly, that monetary policy was purely passive or accommodative and that fiscal policy was the dominant instrument of control or attempted control over rates of total spending in the economy. This seemed to be the appropriate institutional setting for applying public-choice analysis to the Keynesian policy precepts, since this involved using the home turf of the Keynesians themselves. We suggested that the political legacy of Keynes may be summarized in a regime of continuing and apparently mounting budget deficits, inflation, and an expanding public sector.

Those who accept a monetarist paradigm, of almost any variety, may object to this summation. They might acknowledge that the political acceptance of the Keynesian teachings ensures a regime of budget deficits, along with some bias toward public-sector growth. But they would find uncongenial our attribution of inflation to the abandonment of the rule for budget balance. There does exist a monetary authority, and this authority has control powers over the nation's supply of money, quite independently of fiscal action.[3] The Treasury itself cannot strictly turn the printing presses to finance the state's affairs. Within the American institutional setting, it is the central bank, the Federal Reserve Board, that controls the printing press, not the Treasury. Therefore, it might be objected that the linkage between debt-financed deficits and inflation developed in Chapter 7 is too direct, while the linkage between money-financed deficits and inflation treated in the first part of this chapter is based on an analysis that does not incorporate realistic institutional assumptions.

We wish to examine this possible objection in some detail. The monetarists, in their disregard for the impact of alternative institutions on monetary outcomes, have adopted their own version of the "presuppositions of Harvey Road," though with somewhat more justification. Let us assume that there does, in fact, exist a monetary authority, an idealized Federal Reserve Board or central bank, that is totally and completely immune from the pressures of democratic politics. This authority is assumed to be empowered to control the supply of money through the use of any one or any combination of sev-

---

3. David Fand, for instance, rejects the suggestion that the supply of money is endogenous, because he interprets such a proposition as signifying an acceptance of the real-bills doctrine. Our perspective on the endogenous character of the money stock as it relates to budget deficits, however, is quite different and is fully consistent with a monetarist perspective. See David I. Fand, "Can the Central Bank Control the Money Stock?" *Federal Reserve Bank of St. Louis, Review* 52 (January 1970): 12–16.

eral instruments. The decision makers for this authority are assumed to be both wise and benevolent.

Alongside this monetary authority, the political agencies of the national government tax, borrow, and spend.[4] For the reasons discussed in Chapter 7, we should expect the politically oriented decision makers, freed from the time-honored balanced-budget constraint and attuned to the Keynesian teachings, to generate budget deficits and to finance these by public borrowing. This action will tend to distort the public-sector–private-sector allocation of resources in favor of the former. But there need be no direct linkage between debt-financed deficits and inflation because of the control powers of the monetary authority. To simplify our initial discussion here, we may assume that this authority adopts price-level stability as its overriding policy objective.

What will happen when the budget is unbalanced and new debt to finance the deficit is issued by the central government? The Treasury will be required to enter the market and sell bonds to nonbanking institutions and to individuals. This increase in the supply of bonds will reduce bond prices and increase bond yields. In the short run, interest rates generally will rise, which in turn will reduce the rate of private investment. There will be a bias or distortion in the private-sector allocation of resources as between consumption and capital formation, in favor of the former. If the monetary authority does not adopt an accommodative role here and if it sticks to its declared policy objective, the political legacy of Keynesian economics must be modified to read as follows: a regime of budget deficits, a biased increase in the rate of growth in the public sector, a regime of unduly high interest rates, and a slowdown in the rate of private capital formation.

These effects of deficits will remain in all settings, but they will be dampened considerably in an economy that experiences substantial real growth in output over time. In order to keep the price level stable, additional money will be required. Recognizing this, the monetary authority may find itself able to monetize some share of the public debt that the deficit financing of the government creates. Indeed, if there should be some way of limiting the size of budget deficits to the required rate of increase in the supply of money,

---

4. For simplicity here, we may assume that government must borrow in only one type of security. It cannot, by assumption, change the overall "moneyness" of debt by modifying debt structure.

a regime of continuing government deficits in these magnitudes might be deemed acceptable. There would, in this case, remain only a slight bias toward public-sector resource use; other political distortions stemming from the Keynesian teachings would be absent. But the very forces at work to create and to expand budget deficits disproportionately would cause the required limits here to be exceeded, with the consequences noted. At best, growth in real output in the economy through time will reduce the impact of the distortions noted.

The independent monetary authority need not, of course, adopt price-level stability as its single policy objective. The decision makers for this authority may accept some Phillips-curve model in the economy, whether or not this is descriptive of reality, and they may choose some explicit trade-off between inflation and unemployment that they think is attainable. Let us say that they select a 5-percent annual rate of price inflation as a maximally acceptable limit. It is evident that this policy will require a higher rate of growth in the money supply than that required for price-level stability, regardless of the rate of growth in real output in the economy. From this, it follows that the monetary authority can absorb a larger proportion of any government deficit, either directly or indirectly, than it could in the first case. An increasing share of the budget deficit can be monetized as the targeted rate of increase in price levels rises. To the extent that the inflation is explicitly selected as a policy objective of the monetary authority, because of some Phillips-curve weighting of conflicting objectives, the responsibility for achieving the intended result belongs squarely on the authority, and not on the fiscal policy accompaniment. The deficits in the latter provide a convenient means of injecting new money into the economy; they do not, in this setting, cause the new money to be injected. The political biases stemming from the acceptance of Keynesian teachings by those who make fiscal policy decisions are equivalent to those outlined above in the price-stability setting.

The Political Environment of Monetary Policy

The inflationary scenario sketched out above provides us with a convenient bridge between an analysis that presumes the existence of a benevolent and wise set of monetary decision makers and an analysis that incorporates institutional influences on those who make monetary decisions. Suppose that a monetary authority possessing legal powers to influence the stock of money exists in nominal independence of electoral politics. The decision makers for this authority are not, however, required to disclose their objectives for policy. We then observe large and increasing budget deficits, financed nominally by borrowing, while, at the same time, we observe an increasing rate of inflation, made possible by comparable increases in the supply of money. What do we conclude from this plausibly and historically descriptive set of facts? Has the monetary authority explicitly allowed the inflation to occur, basing its choices, rightly or wrongly, on some Phillips-curve model of the economy and choosing some inflation as the appropriate price for attaining higher employment? Or has the authority accommodated its own actions to the same political forces that generated the budget deficits?

What does the recent historical evidence suggest? Do larger deficits tend to elicit increases in the stock of money? Or are changes in the stock of money unrelated to the size of budget deficits? Table 8.1 presents in summary form some pertinent evidence regarding this question. The table covers the twenty-eight-year period, 1946–1974, of which the last half, 1961–1974, corresponds essentially to what we have called the "Keynesian period." During the earlier half of this period, there were six years of budget surplus. During five of these years, the rate of growth in the supply of money was quite low, ranging between −1.3 percent and 1.2 percent. Even during the remaining surplus year, 1947, the rate of money growth was a relatively moderate 3.3 percent. During the remaining eight years, the budget was in deficit. During six of these years, the rate of increase in the money stock exceeded the 1.9-percent average rate of increase over the entire fourteen-year period.

An examination of the 1961–1974 period reinforces the thesis that budget deficits are positively related to changes in the stock of money. During this latter period, the average annual increase in the money stock was 4.9 percent, a full three percentage points above the annual average during the preceding interval. A closer examination of this historical record reveals that the Federal Reserve System has responded to budget deficits (surpluses) by increasing (decreasing) its holding of government securities. This pattern obtains for both the 1946–1960 and the 1961–1974 periods. The Federal Reserve, in other words, appears to be a major source for financing budget deficits. The post-Accord experience seems little different from the situation immediately preceding 1951. What is different is simply that the magnitude of budget def-

Table 8.1 Relation between Budgetary Status and Monetary Change[a]

Calendar year	Budget deficit (−) or surplus (billions of dollars)	Change in Federal Reserve holding of Treasury securities (billions of dollars)	Change in M (billions of dollars)	Change in M (percent)
1947	2.4	−.7	3.6	3.3
1948	3.9	.7	.5	.4
1949	−3.6	−4.4	−1.1	−1.0
1950	−.4	1.9	2.9	2.6
1951	−3.4	3.0	5.1	4.5
1952	−5.8	.9	6.0	5.0
1953	−9.2	1.2	3.1	2.5
1954	−3.7	−1.0	2.0	1.6
1955	−2.8	−.1	4.1	3.1
1956	3.8	.1	1.6	1.2
1957	.6	−.7	.8	.6
1958	−7.1	2.1	1.8	1.3
1959	−7.1	.3	4.4	3.2
1960	1.9	.8	−1.9	−1.3
1961	−6.3	1.5	2.3	1.6
1962	−7.2	1.9	3.0	2.1
1963	−6.7	2.8	4.4	3.0
1964	−8.2	3.4	5.7	3.8
1965	−4.7	3.8	4.4	2.8
1966	−7.3	3.5	3.1	2.2
1967	−14.0	4.8	11.3	6.6
1968	−16.1	3.8	13.1	7.2
1969	7.2	4.3	8.9	4.4
1970	−10.5	4.9	11.1	5.4
1971	−24.8	8.1	13.4	6.2
1972	−17.3	−.3	27.6	12.1
1973	−7.9	8.6	15.7	6.1
1974	−10.9	2.0	13.1	4.8

[a]Source: *Federal Reserve Bulletin* (various issues).

icits has become so immense, and with no offsetting periods of surplus. The "facts" suggest that the actions of the Federal Reserve Board have not been independent of the financing needs of the federal government.[5]

Our hypothesis is that political pressures also impinge on the decisions of monetary authorities, even if somewhat less directly than on elected politicians, and that the same biases toward demand-increasing policy steps will be present. These pressures would be operative even in a balanced-budget regime, let alone in a post-Keynesian world in which elected politicians seem to have abandoned all pretense to balanced-budget norms. That is to say, even if we could imagine modern governments maintaining strict balance between revenue and spending flows, the monetary authorities would be more likely to support inflationary rates of growth in national money supplies than deflationary rates. Such tendencies would be stronger under fractional reserve banking than under 100-percent reserve banking. Expansions in the monetary base by the monetary authority make possible an expansion in credit by individual banks. To the extent that the national monetary authority reflects the interests of the banking community, a fractional reserve system would seem to be more inflationary than a 100-percent reserve system.

In pre-Keynesian periods, when little or no thought was given to departures from principles of "sound finance" by governments, the inflation-proneness of nationally independent monetary authorities was widely accepted. Economists and philosophers used such predictions as the basis of recommendations for automatically operative monetary systems, in which the unit of money was defined by a fixed quantity of a specific commodity (gold being the best example) and with the effective supply being determined by the forces of the market. Historically, monetary systems based on commodity

---

5. The proposition that monetary authorities cannot be treated as truly independent of the financial activities of the Treasury, at least when government expenditure and government debt comprise relatively large parts of national income and total credit respectively, is advanced in R. S. Sayers, *Central Banking after Bagehot* (Oxford: Oxford University Press, 1957), pp. 92–107. Bagehot, by the way, set forth over a century ago (1873) essentially a public-choice–property-rights approach to monetary institutions. See Walter Bagehot, *Lombard Street: A Description of the Money Market*, 11th ed. (London: Kegan, Paul, Trench, Trubner, 1894 [1873]). The importance of relating inflation to politics has recently been stressed by Thomas Wilson, "The Political Economy of Inflation," *Proceedings of the British Academy*, vol. 61 (Oxford: Oxford University Press, 1975), pp. 3–25.

components seemed to be more stable than independent national systems based on fiduciary issue.

Control features comparable in effect to those operative in a commodity standard are imposed on fiduciary systems by internationally fixed exchange rates among currencies. To the extent that money units of one country must be fixed in value by a specific number of units of money of another country, the monetary authority in any one country is severely constrained in its independent power to choose policy targets for purposes of furthering domestic economic objectives.

But consider the position of a monetary authority in an economy that is largely autonomous. The authority is empowered to issue fiduciary currency and to regulate a banking system based on this currency. The authority may be nominally independent of politics, but pressures will, nonetheless, be brought to bear on its operations. What is important for our purposes is that the indirect pressures on the monetary authorities and the direct pressures on politicians will tend to be mutually reinforcing, and especially so in the direction of increases in money growth rates. A monetary decision maker is in a position only one stage removed from that of the directly elected politician. He will normally have been appointed to office by a politician subject to electoral testing, and he may even serve at the pleasure of the latter. It is scarcely to be expected that persons who are chosen as monetary decision makers will be the sort that are likely to take policy stances sharply contrary to those desired by their political associates, especially since these stances would also run counter to strong public opinion and media pressures.

What incentives does a person with decision-making authority in monetary matters have to hold fast to strict neutrality as between demand-increasing and demand-decreasing actions? Public-choice theory incorporates the basic behavioral hypothesis that persons in political and administrative positions of decision-making power are not, in themselves, much different from the rest of us. They tend to be personal-utility maximizers, and they will be influenced directly by the reward-punishment structure that describes their position in the institutional hierarchy. No monetary decision maker, no central banker, enjoys being hailed as the permanent villain of the piece. He does not relish being held up to the public as responsible for massive unemployment, for widespread poverty, for a housing shortage, for sluggish economic performance, and for whatever else that the uninformed and malicious journalist may throw at him. Why should the monetary bureaucrat expose himself to such uninformed but publicly effective abuse when his own decisions take on all of the characteristics of a genuinely "public good."[6] The monetary decision maker may realize full well that there are "social" gains to be secured from adopting and holding firm against demand-increasing, inflation-generating policies. But these general gains will not be translated into personal rewards that can be enjoyed by the decision maker as a consequence of his policy stance. "Easy money" is also "easy" for the monetary manager; "tight money" is extremely unpleasant for him.

The disproportionate acclaims and criticisms of the public, along with the disproportionate likelihood of support and alienation of political associates, suggest that the utility-maximizing monetary decision maker will behave with a natural bias toward inflation. This bias is enhanced when the institutions of a nominally independent monetary authority are themselves thought to be subject to ultimate control and regulation by elected politicians.[7] Consider the role of the monetary manager who takes a "tight money" position, disregarding the public clamor and disregarding the dismay of his political supporters. He can maintain this position only so long as, and to the extent that, his institutional isolation is protected. His position must be tempered severely if he realizes that the legislative authorities can, if pushed, modify the effective "monetary constitution," by imposing specific regulations or, in the limit, by abolishing the independence of the monetary authority itself. Even the most "public spirited" of monetary bureaucrats may, therefore, find himself forced into patterns of behavior that are biased by the disproportionate political pressures, even if these are wholly indirect.[8]

6. Cf. Gordon Tullock, "Public Decisions as Public Goods," *Journal of Political Economy* 79 (August 1971): 913–918.

7. E. Ray Canterbery, *Economics on a New Frontier* (Belmont, Calif.: Wadsworth, 1968), pp. 155–171, explicitly advocates that Federal Reserve nominal independence be replaced by direct political control.

8. There is some empirical evidence to suggest that the behavior of persons in monetary authorities is explained by hypotheses that have emerged from the theory of bureaucracy. See Keith Acheson and John F. Chant, "The Choice of Monetary Instruments and the Theory of Bureaucracy," *Public Choice* 12 (Spring 1972): 13–34; and idem, "Bureaucratic Theory and the Choice of Central Bank Goals," *Journal of Money, Credit, and Banking* 5 (May 1973): 637–655. For a general survey of various efforts to examine positively

To this point, we have continued to assume that the monetary authority operates with confidence in the accuracy of its predictions about movements in economic aggregates, and that it bases its policy actions on well-established and predictable relationships between these and targeted changes in the economic aggregates. This assumption of omniscience must, of course, be replaced by one of partial ignorance and uncertainty. The decision makers must act without full confidence in their predictions, and on the basis of relationships that are not universally acknowledged to be valid. The effect of this uncertainty is to contribute to the inflationary bias already discussed. In a situation of genuine uncertainty, persons will tend more readily to take those decisions that are responsive to external demands.

Autonomous and nominally independent monetary authorities may be biased toward inflation even in a regime in which fiscal policy is guided by the pre-Keynesian precept of budget balance. The presence of debt-financed budget deficits will, moreover, strengthen the tendencies for monetary expansion. Policy steps will be taken to monetize, directly and/or indirectly, some share of the government debt that the demand-increasing fiscal policy makes necessary. In the face of large and increasing budgetary deficits, the achievement of any specified anti-inflation target might require very high interest rates. But rates at this level may not be politically tolerable. Political and public reactions to the increases in interest rates as well as to the high levels may seem to be as severe as, and possibly more severe than, political and public agitation over inflation itself, at least in some anticipated sense. The monetary authority may be held to be more directly responsible for the level of interest rates than for the rate of inflation. Furthermore, the authority may not anticipate that, in subsequent periods, the expected rate of inflation may drive nominal interest rates even higher. In order to maximize their own utilities, considered over a relatively short time horizon, therefore, the monetary decision makers may try to compromise among conflicting objectives. They will tend to look at interest rates and to try to monetize a portion of deficit-induced debt large enough to keep interest rate changes within tol-

---

the conduct of the Federal Reserve authorities, see William P. Yohe, "Federal Reserve Behavior," in William J. Frazer, Jr., ed., *Crisis in Economic Theory* (Gainesville: University of Florida Press, 1974), pp. 189–200.

erable bounds. In the process, they will acquiesce in a rate of monetary growth that causes their anti-inflation targets to be missed.[9]

This scenario might offer both a behaviorally realistic but not totally unacceptable policy set in modern political democracy if we could predict stable magnitudes for the relevant variables. *If* the size of the deficits could be stabilized, or increased only within the limits dictated by the rate of growth in real output, the amount of debt monetization could also be kept within limits, and the rate of inflation could be maintained at some minimal level, to which adjustments could be made over time. There would be some bias toward public-sector allocation, and interest rates would be above noninflationary levels, but they would not be rising over time. Unfortunately, however, the selfsame political forces that might produce the deficit creation–debt monetization–inflationary sequence in the first place will operate to ensure that deficits will continually rise over time. The alleged employment and output stimulation effect of attempted increases in aggregate demand requires increases *from* previously existing levels. If unemployment and excess capacity seem to be present in the economy, and if political decision makers have been fully converted to the Keynesian policy paradigm, they will be persuaded to *increase the size of the budget deficit* on precisely the same argument that might have been successful in convincing their political predecessors to inaugurate a regime of unbalanced budgets. When the Keynesian policy paradigm comes to be embedded in an effectively democratic political process, it generates a dynamic of its own that tends to ensure mounting deficits, with predicted consequences. Even if a nominally independent monetary authority should try initially to immunize itself from political pressures, its attempt must come under increasing strain through time. Permanent insulation of an effective monetary authority from politics is not something upon which hopes for rescue should be based.

9. Several studies of the link between budget deficits and monetary expansion have treated interest rates as the mediator that creates the link. Budget deficits will tend to depress the price of government securities, thereby placing upward pressure on interest rates. The Federal Reserve, in turn, acts to offset this upward pressure by purchasing government securities. In consequence, monetary expansion takes place. For discussions of this point, see Raymond E. Lombra and Raymond G. Torto, "The Strategy of Monetary Policy," *Federal Reserve Bank of Richmond, Monthly Review* 61 (September/October 1975): 3–14; and Susan R. Roesch, "The Monetary-Fiscal Mix through Mid-1976," *Federal Reserve Bank of St. Louis, Review* 57 (August 1975): 2–7.

The corollary of the tendency toward deficits of increasing magnitude over time is the increasing difficulty of securing any reduction in these magnitudes. To a public and to a group of legislators thoroughly converted to textbook Keynesianism, reductions in aggregate spending rates, which might be generated by cutting down on the size of the deficits, will, at any time, cause some increase in unemployment and some cutbacks in real output. Quite apart from the direct and ever-present public-choice reasons that make tax increases and/or expenditure curtailment difficult to achieve, the Keynesian logic offers a strong supporting argument against any such moves for macroeconomic reasons. And in this case, the argument is widely, indeed almost universally, acknowledged to be valid. After a long period of money-financed deficits, growth in the relative size of government, and inflation, any effort on the part of either the budget-making politicians or the monetary authorities to return the national economy toward a regime of balanced budgets, stability in the relative size of the public sector, and price-level stability, will tend to disappoint built-in expectations and will tend to produce the results predicted by the Keynesian models. These embody major costs that are largely concentrated over relatively short periods of time, as against the long-term gains that are promised from the change. Can we really expect ordinary democratic politics to make the difficult decisions required to adopt such a shift of policy? This seems to be the most tragic aspect of the whole Keynesian legacy. A political democracy, once committed to a sequence of Keynesian-motivated money-financed deficits, may find itself incapable of modifying its direction.[10]

The American Political Economy, 1976 and Beyond

The discussion and analysis of Chapters 7 and 8 to this point have employed partially abstracted models of political and economic reality for the purpose of generating predictions about the applicability of Keynesian economics in political democracies. The models have surely been "recognizable" in the sense that they have represented somewhat idealized variants of what we observe as existing institutions. In this concluding section, we wish to relate our

---

10. As Hayek puts it, we may find ourselves caught holding onto a "tiger by the tail." See Friedrich A. Hayek, *A Tiger by the Tail* (London: Institute of Economic Affairs, 1972).

whole analysis more directly and more specifically to the institutions that describe the American political economy in 1976 and beyond. We wish to apply our analytical models and to make predictions about real-world policy changes.

The developing sequence of cumulatively increasing budget deficits has been noted several times, and we need not review this again here. For better or for worse, fiscal policy since the early 1960s has been driven by the Keynesian precepts, as these are transmitted to, interpreted by, and translated into outcomes by elected politicians. The results are those that public-choice models would have allowed us to predict. The Federal Reserve Board exists in nominal independence of direct political pressure, and it is empowered to control the effective supply of money in the economy. Until 1971, the monetary policy of the board was constrained to an extent by the international system of fixed exchange rates among separate major national currencies. Despite the relatively autonomous position of the American economy, because of its magnitude and because of the relative importance of domestic as opposed to international trading, the fixed-rate constraint did serve as an effective brake on expansionary monetary policies in the 1950s and 1960s. Perhaps even more importantly for purposes of our analysis, the fixed-rate constraint offered a means through which the direct political pressures on the monetary authority could be forestalled. Politicians who might otherwise have attempted to reduce the alleged independence of the Federal Reserve Board were prevented from so doing because of the international reserve dangers that inflation might present, the relevance of which could be demonstrated in simple quantitative terms, the loss of gold reserves.

After 1971, and conclusively after 1973, there has been no such constraint on the actions of the Federal Reserve Board, and indirectly on the actions of those politicians who would reduce the board's nominal independence. As a result, the Federal Reserve Board has become more vulnerable to attempts by elected politicians to regulate its activities with respect to money supply. These attempts were successful up to a point in 1975; since that time, the board has been required to announce specific monetary supply targets to the Congress, something that has never been done before. This political pressure on the independence of the Federal Reserve Board continued in 1976. The House of Representatives, early in 1976, overwhelmingly passed a measure that, if finally enacted into law, would substantially curb even the nominal isolation of the board. The measure in question made the term of the chairman of the board coincide with that of the U.S. president and added so-called "public" members to the boards of the regional Federal Reserve banks. Furthermore, the proposed bill directed the board to adopt the maximum employment objectives as specified in the Full Employment Act of 1946.

These observed events, in conjunction with our basic public-choice analysis, leads us to predict that the Federal Reserve Board will come under increasing and perhaps accelerating pressures for more control by the elected political leaders, and that these pressures will gradually come to be more and more effective. Even if this does not directly occur, the fear of potential political dominance will ensure that the decision makers in the Federal Reserve Board will come increasingly to be influenced by the same political pressures that affect those who determine the basic budgetary outcomes.[11]

When we add to this the simple recognition that the Federal Reserve Board is an established bureaucracy, whose members seek to remain secure in their expected perquisites of office, it seems highly unlikely that the Federal Reserve authorities will opt for price-level stability, even as an implicit target for monetary policy. They will accept a rate of inflation as an indirect means of appeasing the political leaders and of assuring them that a share of the newly issued public debt will be monetized. This will, in turn, cause interest rates to rise less rapidly than they might otherwise do in the short term, although the continuing inflationary expectations, which this policy will reinforce, will cause interest rates to remain at high levels over a longer perspective.

This set of predictions may be squared readily with those which have emerged from the more detailed and more sophisticated models that have not incorporated political elements. But our interpretation of the political dynamic of the whole interacting system does not allow us to predict that the American political economy will settle down to some moderate deficit, mod-

11. The revenue collected by government from inflation is quite high, Friedman having estimated it in excess of $25 billion for 1973. Clearly, the forces of government have much to gain from the Federal Reserve's permitting the monetary expansion, so the nominal independence of the Fed should not be allowed to obscure one's understanding of why the expansion takes place under prevailing monetary institutions. The estimate for 1973 is presented in Milton Friedman, *Monetary Correction* (London: Institute of Economic Affairs, 1974), pp. 14–15. For a more general treatment of revenue received by government from inflation, see Milton Friedman, "Government Revenue from Inflation," *Journal of Political Economy* 79 (August 1971): 846–856.

erate inflation, moderate unemployment growth path. Our predictions, based on an attempt to analyze the political forces at work in a post-Keynesian age, and after almost two decades of political Keynesianism, must be less sanguine. This is not to rule out the prospect that, for short periods, attempts may be made seriously to reverse what will become increasingly clear as the trend of events. Indeed, the widespread expression of concern about "fiscal responsibility" in 1975 and 1976 may make possible the temporary political viability of some budgetary restrictions, notably toward holding down the introduction of new expenditure programs. But the analysis of the political forces at work suggests to us that such waves of "reaction," if they occur at all, will tend to be short-lived and to be quickly dominated in significance by the underlying secular realities. The episodic attempts by the Nixon administration in both 1969 and 1973 offer examples that may recur, but probably with less frequency. As others have predicted, the political response that seems likely to occur may make things worse rather than better. Political pressures toward direct controls as a means of keeping inflation within bounds may well become overwhelming, despite the near-universal historical record of failure.

As we have indicated elsewhere in this book, we hope that our predictions are in error. We have attempted to present, first of all, our diagnosis of the American political economy in 1976 and beyond, and to make predictions based on this diagnosis. Few can contemplate the predicted results with other than foreboding. In a sense, we are like the physician whose own diagnosis suggests that his patient has cancer; he would be willing, indeed happy, to acknowledge that he has erred in diagnosis and prediction in exchange for the personally satisfying state of observing that his patient is on the road to recovery and, indeed, may not have been so ill as he seemed. Fortunately, this cancer metaphor is only partially applicable. We know that the patient in our case, the American political economy, can be "cured" by self-restorative steps. The question is one of will. Can the American democracy make the necessary reorganizational arrangements in time to forestall the disasters that now seem to be predictable from its observed post-Keynesian dynamic? This offers the subject matter for most of Part III of this book. Before exploring this question, however, we must first consider carefully the basis for the proposition that particular budgetary institutions can influence budgetary outcomes. We do this because this proposition, while common sense to many, is rejected by a number of professional economists.

9. Institutional Constraints and Political Choice

Introduction

In the preceding two chapters, we have argued that the institutional framework within which fiscal affairs are conducted can and generally will influence the character of fiscal outcomes. Such propositions, however, are opposed strongly by those economists who regard institutions as essentially veils over reality and who assume that individuals will interpret choice alternatives similarly, regardless of the specific form of institutions. In this chapter, we attempt to explain our position more fully.

The question we must ask, and answer, is: Why do citizens support politicians whose decisions yield the results we have described? If citizens are fully informed about the ultimate consequences of alternative policy choices, and if they are rational, they should reject political office seekers or office-holders who are fiscally irresponsible. They should not lend indirect approval to inflation-inducing monetary and fiscal policy; they should not sanction cumulatively increasing budget deficits and the public-sector bias which results. Yet we seem to observe precisely such outcomes.

Since World War II, considerable effort has gone into the development of explanations for the economic activities of government; this book itself falls very much within this tradition, and we first examine briefly some facets of this literature. Next, we consider the ability of tax institutions to alter perceptions of the cost of government, thereby possibly modifying observed budgetary outcomes. Subsequently, we examine debt finance and money finance in turn, focusing on the ability of alternative institutional forms to influence the observed fiscal record.

The Public Economy and the Private

During the decades after World War II, great progress was made toward putting the analysis of the "public economy" on all fours with the more traditional economic analysis of the "private economy." But the additional complexities of the former must always be kept in mind. Persons can be said to "demand" goods and services from government through the political process, and, in many respects, these demands for publicly supplied services may be analyzed similarly to those offered in ordinary private-goods markets.[1] At some basic psychological level of choice, the demand of the citizen for more police protection by the municipality reflects the same drive as his demand for additional door locks from the local hardware store.

Even with such a simple analogy, however, care must be taken lest the similarities be pushed too far. The person who wants to purchase a new lock goes to the local hardware store, or to several stores, surveys the array of alternatives offered for sale, along with the corresponding array of prices, makes his purchase, and is done with it. It should be evident that the person's act of implementing his demand for additional police protection is quite different. The citizen must communicate his desires to his elected political representative, his city councilman, who may or may not listen. If he does listen, the councilman must then take the lead in trying to convince a majority of his colleagues in the representative assembly to support a budgetary adjustment. But what about quality and price? Almost anyone would desire more police protection of high quality if this should be available to him at a zero price. At one level of reaction, the citizen must understand that additional public services can be secured only at the price of either reductions in other services or increases in taxes. How can he indicate to his political representative just what quantity-quality-price mix is most preferred? And how can his political representative, in trying to please his constituents, determine this mix?

Once we so much as begin to ask such questions as these, the complexities in the institutional linkage between the "demands" of citizens for publicly provided goods and services and the final "satisfaction" of those demands by the political structure begin to surface. We shall not attempt a general anal-

---

1. Cf. James M. Buchanan, *The Demand and Supply of Public Goods* (Chicago: Rand McNally, 1968).

ysis here (this is what the rapidly growing subdiscipline of "public choice" is largely about), but some of the basic elements of public fiscal choice must be examined in order to develop our central argument. We seek to show that, by modifying the institutional-constitutional constraints within which fiscal choices are made, Keynesian economics has resulted in different budgetary choices than would have otherwise resulted. Another way of putting our argument in summary form is to say that "institutions matter." Indeed, it is the ability of institutions to matter that transforms the Keynesian legacy into one that has politically undesirable results. If institutions did not matter, voters and their political representatives would behave no differently after the Keynesian destruction of the balanced-budget rule than they behaved before. There would be no asymmetrical application of the Keynesian precepts.

But we must show *why* the institutions of fiscal choice themselves influence the outcomes of that choice. As noted earlier, this may seem intuitively clear to anyone but an economist. To the latter, however, to say that the means of making choices influence outcomes smacks of saying that irrational or nonrational elements of behavior are present. And the economist, true to his guns, may insist that all conceivable models of rational behavior be tested for their explanatory potential before resorting to behavioral hypotheses that embody apparent irrationality. We are both economists, but we do not associate ourselves with the attitude imputed to some of our professional colleagues here, and especially not with reference to individual behavior in fiscal choice.

Fiscal Perception and Tax Institutions

What is rational behavior in fiscal choice? We are not psychologists, but it seems self-evident that individual choice behavior is affected by the costs and benefits of choice alternatives as these are perceived by the chooser, and not as they may exist in some objective dimension necessarily measurable by third parties. The importance of perception in individual choice tends to be obscured in orthodox economic theory, and therefore by economists, for several reasons. For one thing, the choice alternatives in the idealized marketplace are readily identifiable. To the person in the marketplace, an apple is an apple and a dollar is a dollar. Few questions are raised if things are not what they seem. But how would the individual chooser behave if he should confront a barrel of apples of varying quality, not knowing which apple is to be allotted him, and not knowing just what price is to be assigned each apple? This sort of choice setting would begin to approximate that faced by the individual in fiscal choice, and it seems clear that the person's subjective perceptions of benefits and costs which influence his choice will be dependent on the institutions of the choice setting.

It is the *perceptions* of individuals concerning the differential effects of fiscal institutions that are relevant to potential fiscal choice. Empirical evidence abounds to suggest that specialized professional economists are unable to agree on the consequences of many forms of financing budgets. It seems, therefore, reasonable to infer that citizens typically will not possess full knowledge as to how they may be personally affected by changes in fiscal instruments, which is simply to say that they will not interpret their economic experiences in precisely the same manner as a professional economist.

A person receives no partitionable and transferable package or bundle of goods or services from government. And he pays no direct "price" for the access to or utilization of the publicly supplied services that are made available to him by government. Nor does he get a monthly or quarterly bill from government, akin to those that he gets from the electric power company or the telephone company. Payments for publicly supplied services are extracted from a citizen in different ways. His income or earnings may be taxed; commodities that he purchases may be subjected to excise or sales taxes; his property may be assessed for tax purposes; a variety of other activities may be subjected to fiscal charges. In the net, each person will, of course, ultimately be required to give up something of value for government. But this total value will not be independent of his own reactive behavior or of the behavior of others in the community.[2] Furthermore, the individual will never be presented with an expert or outside estimate of the value he pays. He must somehow reckon this total, a process that will be vastly more costly, and dimensionally different, from that which is required to ascertain the prices or costs of goods purchased in private markets.

Different tax institutions will exert differing effects on the individual's perception of his share in the costs of public services. From this, it follows that

2. On this point, see James M. Buchanan, "Externality in Tax Response," *Southern Economic Journal* 33 (July 1966): 35–42.

the form of tax institution, or the tax structure generally, can affect budgetary choices. An individual will prefer smaller (larger) governmental budgets under some tax structures than he will under alternative arrangements. This hypothesis may be accepted, however, without any hypothesis concerning the direction of bias. Will a person desire a smaller or a larger budget under a complex tax structure than he would under a system in which he is sent a monthly bill for all governmental services?

The general proposition that particular individuals make fiscal choices on the basis of their own perceptions and that institutions of choice can, in fact, influence these perceptions may be accepted. But we require an additional step in our argument before we can infer from this that the outcomes of collective choice are directionally biased in one way or the other. So long as the errors in perception made by individuals are distributed symmetrically, or roughly so, around some idealized "true" assessment of alternatives, the model that generally ignores errors in perception will not yield false results. But we suggest that the fiscal perceptions of all persons, or of large numbers, may be systematically biased, that the directional errors are not offsetting, and that we can develop hypotheses concerning the distorting effects of specific fiscal institutions on collective outcomes. "Illusion," quite apart from and in addition to "error," characterizes individual fiscal choices.

It will be helpful to discuss the distinction between "illusion" and "error" in some detail. Models that embody the assumption of behavioral rationality on the part of all actors may yield meaningful predictions if errors in perception are randomly distributed around the "true" mean. In such models, so long as persons at the appropriately defined margins behave in accordance with objectified criteria for rationality, it matters little that persons at either end of the spectrum incorporate nonobjectifiable subjective elements of preference or that they err in their perceptions of the choice alternatives. Institutions may modify the degree to which perceptions are accurate, and, through this, the amount of error in individual fiscal choice. But the amount of error, in itself, is not functionally related to an institutionally induced bias in the collective result of individual choices, a result produced by some voting process. In order to generate such an institutionally induced bias, we must introduce the concept of "illusion," which systematically weights the choice process toward error in a specific direction.

Our summary hypothesis is that complex and indirect payment structures create a fiscal illusion that will systematically produce higher levels of public outlay than those that would be observed under simple-payments structures. Budgets will be related directly to the complexity and indirectness of tax systems. The costs of public services, as generally perceived, will be lower under indirect than under direct taxation, and will be lower under a multiplicity of tax sources than under a system that relies heavily on a single source.

This hypothesis has empirical support, and it seems intuitively plausible.[3] Nonetheless, as noted, it is not readily defended within the corpus of orthodox economic theory. The latter implicitly defines rational behavior in terms of objectifiable magnitudes and, furthermore, embodies the hypothesis that representative persons do not systematically err. The subjectively determined perceptions of persons, which may or may not have counterparts in observable reality, have been neglected.[4] But consider the following setting in which "god" knows that Mr. A will ultimately give up $1000 in value as a result of taxation under either one or two separate institutional forms. Orthodox economic theory could, from this datum, do little other than predict that Mr. A would react similarly under each tax form and, specifically, that his preferred budget would be invariant as between these forms. But Mr. A's budget-level preferences will depend, not on what "god" or some idealized observing economist "knows," but on what he perceives as his own share in the costs of public services. Mr. A is simply not equipped to know more than this.

This much may be accepted; but why will Mr. A perceive costs as lower under the complex than under the simple tax structure? Will he not be as likely to overestimate as to underestimate his tax share? Underestimation is predicted because complexity has the effect of weakening the cost signals, of introducing illusion over and beyond uncertainty. Tax costs, the negative side of individual fiscal choice, are made to seem less than they are.[5] Under a simple tax structure, these cost signals may come through to Mr. A relatively un-

---

3. For a conceptual and empirical examination of the ability of tax institutions to influence the perceived costs of government, thereby modifying budgetary outcomes, see Richard E. Wagner, "Revenue Structure, Fiscal Illusion, and Budgetary Choice," *Public Choice* 25 (Spring 1976): 45–61.

4. The so-called "Austrian school" of economists, along with a more specialized tradition in cost theory centering on the London School of Economics in the 1930s, provide notable exceptions. For a general discussion, see James M. Buchanan, *Cost and Choice* (Chicago: Markham, 1969).

5. For the early treatment of fiscal illusion, see A. Puviani, *Teoria della illusione finanziaria* (Palermo, 1903).

impaired, but under the complex system, such signals may be weak or almost nonexistent at the point where they impact on the psychology of the tax-payer. Perceiving that costs are lower under this alternative, Mr. A will reach marginal adjustment on a preferred level of outlays higher than he would under the simple tax form.

One analytical basis for our contentions about the ability of tax institutions to influence preferred, and through democratic processes actual, budgetary outcomes is related to those found in the psychological literature on information processing.[6] In that literature, it is noted that the degree to which any message is understood varies directly with the strength of the particular signal to be received and inversely with the noise present at the time the signal is transmitted. For instance, a person who is talking with another in a crowded room would tend to hear less accurately what is being said as the volume of the distracting background noise increases. A similar proposition would seem to be reasonable with respect to the interpretation of economic phenomena.[7]

We may introduce the choice situation confronted by a person in a standard market setting as a benchmark here. A price is directly visible in association with a commodity or service bundle of observable quality and quantity dimensions. The cost signal is clear as transmitted, and there is little or no interfering noise.[8] We move somewhat away from this benchmark when we allow, say, the services of a club to be priced as "season tickets." But, even

6. See, for instance, Donald A. Norman, *Memory and Attention* (New York: Wiley, 1969); and Peter H. Lindsay and Donald A. Norman, *Human Information Processing* (New York: Academic Press, 1972).

7. Randall Bartlett makes the same point, only he uses a visual rather than an auditory metaphor. In his framework, some tax forms have higher visibility than others. Starting with perfect visibility, taxes can be arrayed in descending order of visibility. In both his analysis and ours, changes in the institutional format for extracting revenues will influence citizen perceptions of the cost of government. See Randall Bartlett, *Economic Foundations of Political Power* (New York: Free Press, 1973), pp. 92–95.

8. The seminal work on information in a market context is George J. Stigler, "The Economics of Information," *Journal of Political Economy* 69 (June 1961): 213–225. We view our discussion of fiscal information essentially as an extension of Stigler's analysis of market information. Any differences that might seem to exist are those that are necessary to take account of the salient institutional differences between market choice and fiscal choice. Fiscal choice is subject to greater transactional complexity because price quotations are seldom made. Instead, "prices" are typically embedded within a complex network of economic relationships and are unrelated to the purchase of services from government.

here, the signal which states that "you must pay $100 to retain your club membership for next month" remains relatively strong. Something that approaches this might be present if each citizen should receive monthly bills for governmental services. Withholding of payments in advance would, however, weaken somewhat the strength of the cost signal, and also add noise to the system. Consider a message to the effect that "we have withheld $100 from your salary as your share in the costs of the club for last month, but you have $500 left over for yourself." Compare the psychological impact with that of the following message: "You have received $600 in salary, but you owe $100 for club services." Clearly, the first message would generally be regarded as weaker than the second. Not only does the first message transmit or signal the cost of the club's services with less directness, it also does not bring explicitly to mind the alternative to club membership, as the second message does. From this, it follows that under normal conditions, preferred levels of service will be higher in the first institutional instance.

Once we acknowledge the basic point that individual choice behavior depends on individual perceptions of costs and benefits, and that general and systematic biases may be identified, alternative forms of financing payments for governmental services must be acknowledged to modify preferred levels of outlays because of their differing impacts on fiscal perceptions. Indirect taxation, for example, is characterized both by weak signals regarding revenue extraction by government and by a lot of noise stemming from the simultaneous transmission of tax rates and commodity prices. Taxation through inflation might be treated as a particular type of indirect tax, with the signal about the total amount of revenue extracted thoroughly scrambled, along with all sorts of noise being thrown in the system.

The hypothesis that fiscal institutions may affect fiscal perceptions of persons seems plausible enough at first. But economists who insist on pulling the maximum explanatory potential from restricted rationality postulates may not yet be convinced. To this point, we have not allowed for a learning process through which persons might gradually come to be aware of the "true" costs of governmental services, regardless of the forms under which these services are financed. At some final stage at the end of a learning process, at some "behavioral equilibrium," it might be thought that the "true costs" would come home to Mr. A, the representative or median decision maker. And, from this point, he could not be, and would not be, misled by the differential perceptions that differing financing structures seem to generate. With governmental financing, however, there is no "behavioral equilibrium" to-ward which the fiscal process tends to converge, at least in the usual sense familiar to economists. There is no process through which the taxpayer who has operated under fiscal misperceptions can be led to correct his estimates. His situation may be contrasted with that of the consumer who uses credit cards for ordinary market purchases. In this latter case, there may arise initial misperceptions about cost, but when creditors present bills for charges due, the *ex post* estimates of opportunity cost impinge directly and are observable in simple numeraire terms. The consumer has the opportunity to learn, and this will influence future behavior.

With governmental services, however, there is no external entity analo-gous to the creditor in the market example. Under familiar and traditional means of financing governments, tax revenues are collected as the economy operates. There is no incentive for anyone to come back to the taxpayer and present him with estimates as to the actual *ex post* estimates of the cost shares. Nor does the taxpayer himself have an incentive to invest time and resources in making accurate estimates. The "publicness" of the fiscal structure itself reduces the incentive for the person to become informed about his own tax share. Suppose that, upon a sufficient investment of time and other resources, including the acquisition of considerable economic understanding, a tax-payer could reckon his annual share in the costs of government with reason-able accuracy. There is no assurance that the independently acting individual can, himself, secure net gains from such behavior. He is only one participant, one voter, one constituent in a many-person polity. His potential effects on public or political outcomes may be negligible. Recognizing this in advance, the individual taxpayer will not be led to make the required investment in information. He will be fully rational in remaining misinformed, fully ra-tional in allowing his own fiscal choices to be subjected to the whims and fancies of his own perceptions as influenced by the institutions of payment.[9]

Furthermore, the costs of determining individual shares would be prohib-

---

9. This is the fiscal application of one of the general paradoxes or problems of demo-cratic process. If there are large numbers of voters, no one voter has a significant influence on political outcomes. Hence, no voter finds it worthwhile to invest in information, and, in the limit, the individual will not find it advantageous to vote at all. On this, see An-thony Downs, *An Economic Theory of Democracy* (New York: Harper and Row, 1957); and Gordon Tullock, *Toward a Mathematics of Politics* (Ann Arbor: University of Michigan Press, 1967).

itive in many cases, even if there should exist an incentive to make such estimates. Even professional economists are often unable to agree on the consequences of changes in the institutional means of extracting resources from citizens. The continuing and unresolved dispute over the incidence of the corporation income tax is but one illustration. And this inability refers to disagreement over such broad functional categories as consumer prices, factor prices, rents, and profits. Disagreement would be intensified if economists should attempt to impute specific dollar estimates to persons. The economists' proclivity to reduce analysis to mathematical comparison is deceptive here because it conceals the assumption that the taxpayer-arithmetician possesses full knowledge of all the relevant data, and, therefore, understands and interprets economic reality in precisely the same manner as the economist-analyst. But the economist is trained to make certain observations, to see or interpret reality in certain ways, while the experience, training, and interest of most taxpayers is normally quite different. In consequence, few taxpayers would interpret real-world phenomena in a manner identical to that of professional economists, just as few people would sense and understand the transitional character of Tartini's "Sinfonia in A Major" with the acuity of someone possessing some knowledge about Italian baroque music. And we should note that economists themselves are notorious for the variety of their interpretations; as the joke goes: "Put all the economists in the world end-to-end and you would not reach a conclusion." A competitive democracy largely responds to the perceptions of noneconomists, who are predominately ordinary citizens, a consideration that strengthens the presumption that tax institutions will influence budgetary outcomes, and that the directional effects can be subjected to analysis.

Debt-Financed Budget Deficits

Our emphasis in this book is confined to the financing alternatives to current taxation, rather than placed on alternative forms of the latter. This concentration is, of course, owing to our interest in determining the political effects of the abandonment of the quasiconstitutional rule for a strict balanced budget. The more general treatment of the impact of institutions on fiscal choice sketched out above was intended only as introductory to this specific application.[10] Initially, we shall examine the effects of government borrowing as a substitute for current taxation. Following this, we shall consider money creation as the financing device. One of the continuing sources of confusion in economic policy discussion lies in the failure to distinguish carefully between these two distinct methods of financing budget deficits. In part, this is a result of the institutional setting within which genuine money creation is readily disguised as public debt issue (through "sale" of debt instruments to the banking system).

We should note, first of all, that the Keynesian policy principles which call for debt-financed budget deficits are based on an analytical model that purports to demonstrate that current taxation and public debt issue do exert differing effects on the behavior of individuals. That is to say, Keynesian economic theory, in its essentials, embodies the proposition that "institutions matter." In this respect, we are strictly Keynesian, rather than Ricardian in either the classical or the modern application of the converse proposition.

But we must start from scratch, if for no other reason than the existence of unnecessary confusion about simple matters. We are concerned with the effects of genuine government borrowing, and, in order to simplify discussion, we shall confine attention to domestic debt. To finance its budget deficit, government is assumed to sell bonds to its own citizens and to nonbanking institutions within the national economy. The alternative to this deficit-debt policy is budget-balance–current-taxation, with government spending held invariant under the two. How will behavior be different?

THE RICARDIAN THEOREM

David Ricardo explored this question at the beginning of the nineteenth century, and his name is associated with the theorem that holds that tax finance and debt finance are basically equivalent.[11] The imposition of a tax directly

---

10. For a generalized, if still preliminary, treatment of the impact of fiscal institutions on fiscal choices in political democracy, see James M. Buchanan, *Public Finance in Democratic Process* (Chapel Hill: University of North Carolina Press, 1967).

11. David Ricardo, *The Principles of Political Economy and Taxation, Works and Correspondence*, vol. 1, ed. P. Sraffa (Cambridge: Cambridge University Press, 1951), pp. 244–249. In his discussion of the practical political comparison of the tax and debt alternatives, Ricardo did not, himself, adhere to the equivalence theorem. For a discussion of

reduces the net worth of the taxpayer, but the issue of an equivalent amount of government debt generates an equal reduction in net worth because of the future tax liabilities that are required to service and to amortize the debt that is created. Suppose, for example, that the market rate of interest is 10 percent, and that a tax of $100 on a person is replaced by an identical share of a liability that government debt issue embodies, thereby obligating the individual in question to pay $10 per year in interest. The shift between these two financing instruments does not affect the taxpayer's net worth at all. This Ricardian "equivalence theorem" is little more than simple arithmetic in the choice setting of a single person, provided that we assume that there is access to perfectly working capital markets. A person in the position posed by the example here would tend to remain wholly indifferent as to whether government financed its outlays by taxation or by debt since, by assumption, the present value of the fiscal liability is identical under the two alternatives, and, furthermore, the person is assumed to have full knowledge of such equivalence.

To the extent that shifts among the forms of financing might generate differences in the distribution of fiscal liabilities among persons and groups in the economy, the Ricardian theorem may not apply generally.[12] This difficulty can be circumvented by assuming that all persons are equal, at least in respects relevant for aggregative analysis, or that such effects are mutually canceling over the whole community of persons. This allows the analysis to be kept within the choice setting for the single citizen.[13]

Under these restrictions, the equivalence theorem can be generalized beyond the straightforward tax-debt comparison. In its most inclusive variant, the theorem would assert that the particular way in which government ex-

Ricardo's views in some detail, see Gerald O'Driscoll, "The Ricardian Non-Equivalence Theorem," mimeographed (Ames: Iowa State University, April 1976).

12. The prospect that real-world shifts among financing instruments would generate distributional differences provided the basis for Griziotti's attack on the Ricardian theorem. See B. Griziotti, "La diversa pressione tributaria del prestito e dell' imposta," *Giornale degli economisti* (1917).

13. For a modern attempt to apply the Ricardian theorem, without reference to Ricardo, see Robert J. Barro, "Are Government Bonds Net Wealth?" *Journal of Political Economy* 82 (December 1974): 1095–1118. For a criticism of Barro's analysis, see James M. Buchanan, "Barro on the Ricardian Equivalence Theorem," *Journal of Political Economy* 84 (April 1976): 337–342.

tracts resources from the citizen is irrelevant for either private or public choice. Tax finance may be replaced by debt finance; either might be replaced by money creation; an income tax might be replaced by a sales tax. So long as the governmental outlay to be financed is the same in each case, and so long as this outlay is shared among persons in the same way, there are no effects on final outcomes. The theorem rests on the basic presumption that the representative decision maker has perfect knowledge about how changes in the means of financing government will affect his own worth. If, in such a setting for analysis, the alternatives are presented so as to ensure that the arithmetical value of the fiscal charge is identical under varying instructional forms, it is no wonder that the precepts of rationality dictate indifference among them.

THE KEYNESIAN PROPOSITION

The Ricardian theorem seems unacceptable because of its neglect of the informational requirements for the behavioral responses that it postulates. We shall return to a more concrete criticism of the debt-tax comparison at a later point, but we shall first contrast the Ricardian with the Keynesian proposition to the effect that debt-financed budget deficits offer an almost ideal instrument for changing individual behavior, for inducing desired increases in aggregate spending during periods of economic slack.

In its early and most naive formulations, the Keynesian model related consumption spending directly to current disposable income. Since taxes represent reductions from total income receipts before disposition, it follows more or less mechanistically that a reduction in taxes will increase the rate of current spending on consumption. But someone must purchase the bonds, someone must surrender the current purchasing power which will allow government to replace tax financing of its outlays (we do not allow money creation in this model). This presents no problem in the initially assumed Keynesian setting. Bonds are purchased with funds drawn from idle hoards; interest rates are not changed; investment spending is not directly affected. The overall effect of the shift from tax-financed budget balance to debt-financed deficits is to increase the rate of total spending in the economy.

In this setting, interest rates are at their floors. Hence, bonds can be marketed on highly favorable terms by the government. (Of course, in the strict sense, no interest rate at all should be paid in this set of conditions. But this would amount to money creation, an alternative that will be specifically discussed below.) So long as any positive rate of interest is paid, however, the Ricardian challenge could have been made. So long as individuals are fully rational in their behavior, so long as they base current decisions on present values of future income streams, the fiscal policy shift under examination here, the shift from tax to bond financing, will not influence behavior. The most central proposition in the Keynesian policy package seems vulnerable to attack on the economists' own grounds.

Retrospectively, it is surprising that such an attack or challenge was not launched soon after Keynesian ideas were presented to economists. Almost universally, economists accepted the Keynesian proposition that debt-financed deficits would increase total spending in the economy. The unquestioning acceptance of this proposition remained long after the naive Keynesian model was amended to allow asset values along with income flows to influence spending decisions. Government debt instruments were treated as positively valued assets in the national balance sheet, but little or no attention was paid to the Ricardian notion that the future tax payments embodied in public debt may also represent liabilities. There was no early Keynesian discussion, in support or in opposition, of the hypothesis that the possible efficacy of fiscal policy depends on the presence of some sort of "fiscal illusion."

This now-apparent neglect or oversight stemmed, in large part, from the Keynesian "theory" of public debt itself, to which we have already made frequent reference. In their early enthusiasm for policy adherence by politicians and the public, Keynesian economists sought to undermine traditional and time-honored "public principles" about the temporal incidence of public debt financing. This zeal, combined with the Keynesian willingness to discuss movements in aggregative economic components without reference to underlying individual choices, along with the confusion between debt financing and money creation, prompted widespread espousal of the basically absurd notion that there is no "burden" of domestic public debt. Such a notion was not, in its origins, specifically Keynesian. It had been variously advanced many times in opposition to the classical principles of public debt, but the "no burden" argument achieved the status of economic orthodoxy only with the surge of development in macroeconomic theory after World War II. Since, according to this "theory," the issue of debt imposes no burden on future taxpayers, there would hardly have been any attention paid to the question concerning possible net capitalization of future tax liabilities in such a way as to influence spending behavior in the periods when debt is issued. The payment of interest to bond holders can be made from taxes, and these taxes may, of course, be capitalized and treated as current liabilities. But since such taxes are collected for the purpose of paying interest to domestic holders of bonds, these interest receipts may also be capitalized into current asset values, just matching the liabilities that the tax payments reflect. In the net, these effects cancel, leaving the initial spending impact of the debt-financing operation unaffected by present-value computations. This no-burden scenario is erroneous because it fails to include the drawing down of private assets when public debt instruments are purchased. But it is not our purpose here to criticize the Keynesian theory of public debt in depth or detail.[14] The summary sketch is included only to suggest that only by understanding the corollary or complementary theory of public debt can we "explain" the Keynesian neglect of the potential Ricardian challenge.

A PUBLIC-CHOICE, POST-KEYNESIAN SYNTHESIS

As we noted, we are not Ricardians. Pure fiscal policy can exert effects on the behavior of the citizen-taxpayer. To this extent, our analysis is in agreement with the Keynesian. But we must go beyond this and see just how the choice situation is changed. The replacement of current tax financing by government borrowing has the effect of reducing the "perceived price" of governmental goods and services. This "relative price" change embodies an income effect of the orthodox Hicksian sort, and this income effect will generate some attempted increase in the rate of private spending. This is essentially the Keynesian result. Note that we need not require the total absence of a Ricardian recognition of future tax liabilities. Citizens-taxpayers may anticipate the future taxes that are implicit with government borrowing, but, in

---

14. For further development, see James M. Buchanan, *Public Principles of Public Debt* (Homewood, Ill.: Richard D. Irwin, 1958); James M. Ferguson, ed., *Public Debt and Future Generations* (Chapel Hill: University of North Carolina Press, 1964); James M. Buchanan and Richard E. Wagner, *Public Debt in a Democratic Society* (Washington: American Enterprise Institute, 1967); and E. G. West, "Public Debt Burden and Cost Theory," *Economic Inquiry* 13 (June 1975): 179–190.

doing so, they need not value these at the extreme Ricardian limits. To the extent that the costs of governmental goods and services are perceived to be lowered by any degree through the substitution of debt for tax finance, the "relative-price" change will be present.

Our emphasis is not, however, on the income effect of this change, and on the influence of this income effect on attempted rates of private spending. Our emphasis is on the more direct substitution effect of the relative-price change, an effect that seems to have been almost totally neglected in the Keynesian discussion. Debt financing reduces the perceived price of publicly provided goods and services. In response, citizens-taxpayers increase their demands for such goods and services. Preferred budget levels will be higher, and these preferences will be sensed by politicians and translated into political outcomes.[15] The constraints placed on elected political representatives against increasing current taxes are dramatically modified by the debt issue option. The possibility of borrowing allows these politicians to expand rates of spending without changing current levels of taxation. Empirically, the record seems clear: The increase in future taxation that public debt implies will not generate constituency pressures comparable to those generated by increases in current taxation.

THE INCENTIVE STRUCTURE OF DEBT FINANCE

These matters of citizen knowledge are compounded by matters of incentive. In the Ricardian setting, each citizen is assigned a known obligation for future debt amortization. In this setting, one can choose between a one-time levy of $1000 or a perpetual annual payment of $100. At a 10-percent rate of discount, these two means of payment are actuarially equivalent. For this actuarial equivalence to generate behavioral equivalence, however, the debt encumbrance should exist as part of an ownership claim to transferable wealth.

---

15. For empirical support of this proposition, developed from an examination of the impact of alternative debt-tax mixes for a set of cities in New York, see Kenneth V. Greene, "An Empirical Test of the Wagner Debt Illusion Hypothesis," in *Issues in Urban Public Finance* (Saarbrucken: International Institute of Public Finance, 1973), pp. 208–225. Related empirical support is found in Wallace E. Oates, " 'Automatic' Increases in Tax Revenues—The Effect on the Size of the Public Budget," in Wallace E. Oates, ed., *Financing the New Federalism* (Baltimore: Johns Hopkins Press, 1975), pp. 139–160.

A perpetual encumbrance on, say, a house would reduce the present market value of that house by the full capital amount.

Such transferability does not exist, however, for encumbrances that result through debt creation by a national government. A taxpayer is not required to purchase an exit visa before he can die. He does not have to undergo a final reckoning for his debt choices. Only if the taxpayer should regard his heirs as lineal extensions of himself would debt choices produce the same behavioral incentives as would the placing of encumbrances on transferable capital assets.

Consider again the choice between a current tax of $1000 and a perpetual debt service charge of $100 annually, with a market rate of interest of 10 percent. For a person with forty years of taxpaying life remaining, the present value of his debt service payments would be $977.89, or 97.8 percent of the cost of government under tax finance. By contrast, for someone with only ten years of taxpaying life remaining, the cost of government under debt finance would be only 61.4 percent of the cost under tax finance. And someone with a taxpaying life expectancy of twenty years—roughly a median position in contemporary America—government would be only 85.1 percent as costly under debt finance as it would be under tax finance.

The nontransferable character of the encumbrances represented by public debt, then, creates incentives for increased public spending under debt finance.[16] Insofar as life-cycle considerations enter at all into the planning of individuals, the present value of any future stream of tax payments will depend on the age of the taxpayer, on his position in his own life cycle. An elderly taxpayer, for example, so long as he is less interested in the present value of the tax liabilities that a current issue of debt will impose on his descendants than he is in the present value imposed on him personally, will regard debt finance as lowering the price he must pay for public services, thereby desiring a larger public budget under debt finance than under tax finance.

---

16. Local finance, in contrast to national finance, possesses transferability of encumbrances, at least to the extent that revenues are raised through property taxation and voters are owners of property in the locality. Even in this setting, however, there may be some tendency toward excessive debt creation, for reasons developed in Richard E. Wagner, "Optimality in Local Debt Limitation," *National Tax Journal* 23 (September 1970): 297–305.

And the extent of this reduction in price will vary directly with the age of the taxpayer.

The position of the fully informed, fully rational taxpayer at the other end of the age spectrum will, of course, be different. The predicted years of personal tax liability may be sufficiently numerous to convert such a person into a Ricardian actor. But this will take place only in the limiting case. And, even in such a setting, the young taxpayer will reach a position where he is indifferent as between the debt and the tax alternative. His fiscal choices under the two instruments will, in this limit, remain invariant.

Consider the combination of pressures that will be brought to bear on the elected politicians who must represent all age groups. Will these pressures, to which we predict the politician to respond, suggest that he opt for more, the same, or less public spending under unbalanced budgets than under balanced budgets? The answer seems clear. To the younger members of his constituency, there will be, in the limit, no pressures for differentiation. Their preferred levels of budgetary outlay will remain unchanged as debt is substituted for current taxation, provided, of course, we stay within the strict confines of the full-information model here. The older members of the politician's constituency will, however, clearly express a bias toward higher levels of spending under the debt alternative. The one group is, in the limit, neutral; the other has a rationally motivated directional bias. The net pressures on the politicians clearly tend toward expanded spending, with the "unrepresented" being those yet-unfranchised future taxpayers who must bear the liabilities chosen by their ancestors.

The predicted effects of debt financing on budget levels are not, of course, new results that emerge only from a public-choice analysis of politics. It is precisely because such effects were widely predicted to characterize the behavior of ordinary politicians that the classical principles of "sound finance" were deemed to be important enough to translate into specific institutional constraints. The predicted proclivities of politicians to spend unwisely unless they are required simultaneously to impose taxes offer the bases for the existence of the balanced-budget norm in the first place. Without general and traditional acceptance of such predictions, we should scarcely have observed such institutions as debt limits, sinking funds, and capital budgeting. The events of fiscal history strongly support the hypothesis that unconstrained access to public borrowing will tend to generate excessive public spending.

The Keynesian policy prescriptions require the removal of all such institutional-constitutional constraints, at least at the level of the central or national government. Indeed, the central Keynesian aim was that of securing increased private spending by way of the increased public spending that deficit financing makes possible. The lacuna in the Keynesian prescription is the absence of some counterforce, a control or governor that will keep public spending within limits.

Money-Financed Budget Deficits

Central governments possess an alternative to debt as a means of financing budget deficits. They can create money which may be used directly to cover revenue shortfalls. In fact, much of what is ordinarily referred to as "public debt" really represents disguised monetary issue by central banks.

How does this institution affect our analysis of budget imbalance? In the non-Keynesian world, the inflation generated directly by the money created to finance a budget deficit is analytically equivalent to a tax, and many economists have examined it in these terms.[17] In terms of the fiscal perceptions of citizens, however, inflation does not seem at all equivalent to a tax. No explicit political discussion and decision takes place on either the source or the rate of tax to be imposed. Individual citizens are likely to be less informed about the probable costs of an "inflation tax" than they are about even the most indirect and complex explicit levy.[18]

17. We do not propose to review this discussion of inflation as a form of tax. For a sample of this literature, see Milton Friedman, "Government Revenue from Inflation," *Journal of Political Economy* 79 (July/August 1971): 846–856; Reuben A. Kessel and Armen A. Alchian, "Effects of Inflation," *Journal of Political Economy* 70 (December 1962): 521–537; and Martin J. Bailey, "The Welfare Cost of Inflationary Finance," *Journal of Political Economy* 64 (April 1956): 93–110.

18. Quite apart from the largely unperceived "tax on cash" which inflation represents, there is an additional element at work which serves to increase real tax rates, thereby generating automatic increases in budgetary levels. If incomes are taxed at progressive rates, and if such components as the tax base, rate brackets, and provisions for exemptions, deductions, and credits are defined in nominal monetary units, real rates of tax will rise with inflation even with no change in real income. In the absence of overt political action to reduce nominal rates of tax, governmental spending in real terms will necessarily rise. For a development of this point, see James M. Buchanan, "Inflation, Progression, and Poli-

The tax signal under inflation is overwhelmed by the accompanying noise which takes the form of rising prices, at least under prevailing institutional arrangements. Psychologically, individuals do not sense inflation to be a tax on their money balances; they do not attribute the diminution of their real wealth to the legalized "counterfeiting" activities of government. Rather, the sense data take the form of rising prices for goods and services purchased in the private sector. The decline in real wealth is attributed to failings in the market economy, not to governmental money creation. It is a rare individual (not one in a million, according to Keynes) who is able to cut through the inflation veil and to attribute the price increases to government-induced inflation produced by the monetary financing of budget deficits. Inflationary finance, then, will generally produce an underestimation of the opportunity cost of public services, in addition to promoting a false attribution in the minds of citizens as to the reason for the decline in their real wealth, a false attribution that nonetheless influences the specific character of public policies.

This informational bias of inflationary finance may be made even more convincing by considering two alternative institutional means for governmental money creation. Consider a commodity-standard system in which the monetary commodity takes on a powered form. In one setting, the sovereign periodically goes from house to house, confiscating a portion of each person's monetary commodity. Under this institutional arrangement, individual citizens, it would seem, would sense clearly that they were being taxed by the sovereign to finance his activities.

Now consider an institutional arrangement in which the sovereign merely adulterates the monetary commodity by adding a quantity of an identically appearing substance to the monetary power that passes through his hands. This alternative institutional means of inflationary finance would produce

---

tics," in *Inflation, Economic Growth and Taxation, Proceedings of the 29th Session (1973), International Institute of Public Finance* (Barcelona: Ediciones Alba, S.A., 1975), pp. 45–46. For an empirical examination of the actual extent of such increases in real tax rates, see Charles J. Goetz and Warren E. Weber, "Intertemporal Changes in Real Federal Income Tax Rates, 1954–70," *National Tax Journal* 24 (March 1971): 51–63. For empirical evidence supporting the thesis of underestimation of taxation that results from inflation, with the result being a rise in public expenditure, see Oates.

signals, regarding the cost of government to citizens, substantially different from those that would be produced by the former arrangement. In the latter case, the one that corresponds to contemporary practice, the sovereign is un-obtrusive; only private businessmen are obtrusive, and it is they who appear to be the source of the decline in net wealth suffered by individual citizens. The ability of such a sovereign to adulterate the money stock, then, would reduce the perceived cost of government, thereby promoting an expansion in the size of the public sector.[19]

Institutions Matter

The ability of institutions systematically to influence perceptions and, consequently, choices seems straightforward once the orthodox, neoclassical framework is rejected. A primary characteristic of this orthodox framework is the presumption, largely for reasons of analytical convenience, that the nature of economic reality is assumed to be fully known or, put more carefully, that models based on such an assumption yield fruitful predictions. So long as analysis is confined to such models, it is not at all surprising that there is no scope for institutions to matter. Who but an ivory-tower economist, however, would be willing to restrict analysis in this way? Once it is recognized that each person must form his own interpretation about the nature of economic reality (such an interpretation is not given to us from on high), it becomes simple to see that institutions will normally influence choices and that such influence can be analyzed.

19. This simple contrast does not deny that people can come to anticipate changes in the price level, the value of money, and react accordingly in their market transactions. Anticipations of inflation may form more rapidly under the first institution than under the second, but, under both institutions, we would expect to observe shifts in the nominal terms of trade in market transactions. What is different as between the two institutions is the informational setting for public choice.

PART THREE

What Can Be Done?

10. Alternative Budgetary Rules

As our previous citation from Hugh Dalton suggests, the early Keynesian emphasis was directed toward the use of the governmental budget to "balance the economy," rather than toward the old-fashioned objective of balancing the government's own fiscal account. The nexus between governmental outlays and the willingness of members of the public to undergo the costs of these outlays was jettisoned. Taxes were to be levied only for the purpose of preventing inflation.

These early Keynesian views took form in the precepts of "functional finance," the unadulterated Keynesian substitute for the principle of the annually balanced budget.[1] A government that followed the precepts of functional finance should let the state of its budget be determined wholly by the needs of national macroeconomic management. Budget surpluses would be incurred to curb inflationary pressures, and budget deficits would be created when unemployment appeared. There was no acknowledgment in this early Keynesian discussion that inflation might, in fact, show up before satisfactorily "full" employment is attained, a situation for which the principles of functional finance offered no obvious policy guidance. This aside, however, the focal point of governmental activity under functional finance was the stabilization of prices and employment.

In contrast, the focal point under the balanced-budget principle was the provision of various goods and services through government. The balanced-budget principle, however, was never operationally replaced by an accepted regime of functional finance. Very few economists (and even fewer politicians) were willing to go to the extreme limits suggested by functional fi-

---

1. The seminal exposition of functional finance is Abba P. Lerner, "Functional Finance and the Federal Debt," *Social Research* 10 (February 1943): 38–51.

nance. Hence, various intermediate principles emerged that attempted to achieve a truce between the implied Keynesian norms of functional finance and the old-fashioned precepts of the balanced budget. In this chapter, we shall describe these various replacements for the balanced-budget norm. Accumulating experience indicates that the constraining impact of these alternative principles has been frail indeed.

Budget Balance over the Cycle

The principle that the government's budget should be balanced over the course of the business cycle represented an effort to bridge the gulf that appeared to separate the Keynesian precept of functional finance from the classical precept of an annually balanced budget. Budget balance over the cycle appeared to retain an ultimate balancing of revenues and outlays, of costs and benefits, which is the essential feature of the strict budget-balance concept. The old-fashioned rule was to be modified only in the accounting period over which the balancing criterion was to be applied; the period was lengthened from the arbitrary accounting year to that which described the full sequence of the business cycle. It appeared that this would allow for the discretionary use of the budget for purposes of countercyclical macroeconomic management. The modified old-fashioned rule and the new Keynesian use of the budget looked to be fully harmonious.

This apparent reconciliation of these two sets of budgetary principles would possibly have been successful if, in fact, business cycles were somehow known to be regular in their amplitude and time sequence and, in addition, were known to exist exogenous to economic policy. In this situation, and only in this situation, business activity would rise and fall with a regular and predictable rhythm. Budget deficits and surpluses could be applied symmetrically, and the amplitude of the fluctuations could be diminished. The deficits and surpluses would cancel out over the entire cycle, and yet macroeconomic management would smooth out both the peaks and the troughs of economic activity. When business cycles occur in a predictable pattern of regular oscillations and when political constraints on budgetary policy are ignored, the principle of a balanced budget over the cycle seems to bridge the gulf that otherwise would seem to separate the classical and the Keynesian prescriptions.

Even if the underlying oscillations in economic activity were known to be regular and exogenous, this budgetary rule would probably be applied asymmetrically in a democratic setting, for reasons we have already developed in Chapter 7. Once the irregularity and subsequent nonpredictability of cycles are acknowledged, this political bias would become even stronger. However, in a setting in which cyclical swings are *known* to be regular, the presence of a cumulative budget deficit over the whole cycle would offer a clear and unambiguous indicator that the balancing rule had been violated. Knowledge that such a criterion might be present would itself act as a constraint on irresponsible budgetary behavior. When cycles are irregular, however, the rule for a cyclically balanced budget and that for functional finance are inconsistent, quite independent of political bias in application. One has to give way to the other. Either the cyclically balanced budget must be pursued at the expense of functional finance, or functional finance must take precedence over the norm of a cyclically balanced budget. The irregularity of cycles undermines the bridge between the two norms and, therefore, negates the possibility that the rule of budget balance over the cycle could serve as an effective substitute for the constitutional constraint of budget balance within the accounting period.

The principle of a balanced budget over the cycle, which acknowledged the necessity for budgetary manipulation to achieve common stabilization objectives, had a relatively short existence in the arsenal of fiscal weapons. A line of argument soon surfaced to suggest that prevailing budgetary-fiscal institutions operated automatically to stabilize the aggregate level of economic activity. This idea of built-in flexibility shifted the focus from the need for discretionary fiscal manipulation to the prospects for institutional adjustments that would ensure automatic fiscal reactions in the direction of desired objectives.

Built-in Flexibility

As our narrative in earlier chapters has shown, one of the first steps on the way to full-fledged Keynesian budgetary management was the recognition that attempts to maintain strict budget balance during periods of economic distress might accentuate depression and, in turn, worsen rather than improve the prospects of budget balance. It was noted that the deficits of the early depression years of the 1930s were due to the simultaneous fall in tax revenues and the increase in relief outlays, and that these deficits themselves were forces leading toward recovery. Before the 1930s, when strictly classical principles were dominant, such "built-in flexibility" was considered to be an undesirable property of a fiscal system. Instability in revenues and outlays was something to be avoided, since this made the task of balancing the budget more difficult. With the deficits of the Great Depression, however, there came to be increasing awareness that such instability was desirable in itself. Macro-economic considerations began to emerge, and built-in flexibility was adjudged to moderate fluctuations in aggregate economic activity.[2]

Once these side effects of budgetary unbalance were fully recognized to be desirable, a natural extension, and especially to those economists who had accepted the then new Keynesian paradigm, was to propose structural changes in the budget that would increase the macroeconomic adjustments, that would increase the built-in flexibility. That is to say, Keynesian-inspired norms for both the taxing and the spending structure appeared alongside the traditional norms which were derivative from considerations internal to the fiscal system rather than external. Proposals for tax reform came to be evaluated against macroeconomic criteria, for their effects on real income and employment, over and above those familiar criteria of "justice," "equity," "convenience," "certainty," and others. In some cases, the macroeconomic criteria achieved dominance in the economists' lexicon. Similar changes occurred in the analysis of spending. Macroeconomic arguments, based on Keynesian economics, came to be advanced for the acceleration of welfare and relief types of budgetary outlay.

In their early phases, however, the policy implications of these arguments for built-in flexibility were confined to structural features on both the revenue and spending sides of the fiscal account. There was nothing here that offered a norm or criterion for the state of budget balance or imbalance. In one sense, the discovery of built-in flexibility, both in its positive and in its normative aspect, was supplemental to the accompanying discussion of alternatives to the balanced-budget rule.

---

2. See Herbert Stein, *The Fiscal Revolution in America* (Chicago: University of Chicago Press, 1969), pp. 187–190, for a discussion of the change in attitudes toward built-in flexibility which took place during the 1930s.

Budget Balance at Full Employment

The incorporation of the structural norms for built-in flexibility provided almost a natural lead-in to an alternative to that of the annually balanced budget. This alternative is the principle of budget balance at full employment, or, as it has come to be known in the 1960s and 1970s, budget balance at high employment. Once it came to be recognized that the budget deficits that emerged passively during periods of economic recession exerted desired pressures toward recovery, it was but a small step to the recognition that the recovery itself exerted a simultaneous effect on the size of the deficits. From this, it followed that the expansiveness or the restrictiveness of fiscal policy might be measured, not by looking at the generation of surpluses or deficits in any current-period setting, but by predictions of the effects that would emerge in a hypothetically postulated setting of full employment.[3] In the Keynesian economic environment, if the economy is operating at full employment, there is no Keynesian-inspired reason for departure from budget balance. The norm should become, therefore, that of setting revenues and expenditures such that the two sides of the budget will come into balance if the full-employment level of income should be achieved. Under the operation of this norm, and because of the built-in flexibility, surpluses would automatically be created in all settings in which demand pressures are excessive. This alternative rule seems to incorporate both the norms for Keynesian budgetary management and the classical principle of balancing revenues against spending. In particular, the fiscal choice process, in the Wicksellian emphasis, seems to be balanced here in that new programs of spending proposed would be weighed against the tax costs of these programs, at full-employment income.

The analytical basis of the budget-balance-at-full-employment rule is starkly simple. Assume, for purposes of argument here, that federal budget outlays are currently at an annual rate of $400 billion, and that tax collections are at the annual rate of $350 billion. In current account terms, there is a budget deficit of $50 billion on an annualized basis. Suppose, however, that the economic situation is also characterized by an unemployment rate of 7 percent, clearly adjudged to be a less-than-full-employment rate.

---

3. See Stein, pp. 127–128, for a discussion of the emergence of this idea.

Now assume further that it is predicted that a fall in the unemployment rate (i.e., an increase in real income and employment) acts both to increase tax collections (because of the increase in income) and to reduce somewhat the rate of federal spending (on unemployment compensation, on food stamps, on relief payments). Let us say that it is predicted that a 2-percent shift in the unemployment rate, to 5 percent, will increase tax revenues to $390 billion and will cut spending to $390 billion. The $50 billion budget deficit, now observed, would vanish and the budget would be in balance. But what if "full employment" is defined to be 4 percent? The budget would have reached balance at the 5-percent unemployment rate. If unemployment should be reduced to 4 percent, further operation of the built-in stabilizers would generate total revenues at a predicted $410 billion rate, and outlays would be predicted to fall to $385 billion. Hence, at the defined full-employment rate of 4 percent, the federal budget would be in *surplus,* not in deficit. The initially observed $50 billion shortfall in revenues behind outlays would actually be indicative of a "full-employment surplus." Politicians, the public, and the professors might then talk themselves into thinking that a fully responsible fiscal policy would require *increasing* the observed deficit.

"Full-employment surplus," a phrase that became prominent in the Economic Report of the President's Council of Economic Advisers after 1962, is the difference between anticipated federal revenues and federal government outlays or expenditures that are projected at some arbitrarily designated level of employment and income.[4] As early as 1947, the Committee for Economic Development proposed that the federal budget should be arranged so that a $3 billion surplus would emerge at an unemployment rate of 4 percent.[5] This particular projection also yielded a balanced budget at an unemployment rate of 6 percent. In this framework, any given budget is considered to be expansive if the full-employment surplus is negative, and contractionary if this full-employment surplus is positive. The larger the surplus, the more restrictive the budget structure is considered, regardless of the fact that actual

4. For a description of the technique used to estimate full-employment surplus, see Keith Carlson, "Estimates of the High-Employment Budget, 1947–1967," *Federal Reserve Board of St. Louis, Review* 49 (June 1967): 6–14.

5. *Taxes and the Budget: A Program for Prosperity in a Free Economy* (New York: Committee for Economic Development, 1947). See also Walter W. Heller, "CED's Stabilizing Budget Policy after Ten Years," *American Economic Review* 47 (September 1957): 634–651.

budget may be running a substantial deficit. Similarly, the more negative the full-employment surplus, the more expansive the budget is considered, regardless of the actual, contemporaneous relation between taxes and expenditures.

The conception of budget balance at full employment has wide support, and, as a norm, it might appear to be a reasonable compromise between the old-time fiscal religion and the Keynesian precepts. The implied norms for budget balance at full employment seem to meet minimal classical requirements while allowing functional finance to operate. This service to two masters might be pardonable if the principle should be able to achieve its logical promise in practice. But it should be clear that this promise will not likely be met. Politically, what appears to be a vehicle to promote fiscal responsibility may become little more than an excuse for the budgetary license. Quite apart from the political implications, however, the whole conception is deceptive in its unacknowledged dependence on the existence of the presumed economic environment of the 1930s.

We shall initially examine the possible application of this principle independently of the political- or public-choice biases that emerge in exaggerated form under its influence. To do so, we may assume that democratic political pressures exert no influence on fiscal decisions, which are made exclusively by "wise" persons in Washington. This is, of course, a wholly unrealistic setting for fiscal policy choices, but it helpfully allows us to isolate the fundamental economic implications of this proposed alternative rule for budget making.

The rule is deceptive because it tends to conceal the implicit assumption about the state or condition of the economy that it contains. This is that the national economy resembles the economy of the early Keynesian models. In these, as we have previously noted, "full-employment income" is sharply and clearly defined; expansions in total spending exclusively affect real output and employment until this level of income is attained; there is no upward pressure on prices. These naive models have substantially disappeared from sophisticated economic discourse, but it is perhaps a mark of the distance between the realm of ideas and that of practice that these naive models seem to persist beneath the surface of most current discussions of the full-employment surplus.

In earlier chapters, we traced the history of the changes in economists' attitudes as these naive models were replaced by those that embodied the Phillips-curve sort of trade-off between unemployment and inflation. A specific definition for "full-employment income" does not emerge from the trade-off models, and macroeconomic policy of any kind requires the selection of some point on a curve which is seen as continuous, with no kinks or corners. But what does this do to the rule for budget balance at full employment? The dilemma has, of course, been recognized, and attempts have been made to rescue the efficacy of the widely accepted principle for fiscal "responsibility" by specifying some combined unemployment-inflation targets. These have ranged from the more restrictive norm of "budget balance at that level of income and employment that can be achieved without inflation" to the norm that simply defines an employment target, say 4-percent unemployment, and disregards the potential inflationary consequences.

What is relevant for our purposes is that any such combination of targeted levels of unemployment and inflation reflects an explicit selection of an arbitrary point along an alleged inflation-unemployment trade-off curve. As such, there is no demonstrably unique point that dominates all others, and reasonable persons may differ concerning the relative weights to be assigned to the two conflicting objectives, increased employment and reduced inflation. Assignment of the decisions to "wise" persons will in no way remove the necessity of establishing some weights.

Economists in increasing numbers have gone beyond even the simplistic trade-off models, however, and it is now widely acknowledged that a Phillips curve, even if one exists, will shift through time as expectations are modified. What does this do for the potential applicability of the "budget balance at full employment" rule? Suppose, for example, that a combination of a 4-percent unemployment rate and a 4-percent rate of inflation is selected as the objective for policy, as the economic setting for which an attempt would be made to bring federal government revenues and outlays into balance. Suppose, further, that this combination does, in fact, describe a possible position for the economy at the time the target is selected, say, in 1977. Let us say that budgetary plans for 1978 and 1979 are then made on the basis of this target, and budgetary authorities rearrange institutions of taxing and spending to this end (such decisions are now made, we assume, by the bureaucrats appointed by the wise persons). But this whole procedure, to be at all workable, depends on the stability of the presumed Phillips curve, on the attainability of the 4–4 points. Suppose, however, that, by the time the budgetary adjustments take effect, by 1979, the Phillips curve has shifted, and the rate of inflation that will emerge at a 4-percent unemployment rate is 6 percent, rather than the 4 percent incorporated in the plans. The emptiness of the proposed norm for budgetary management becomes apparent.[6]

At the extreme other end of the spectrum from the early naive Keynesian models in which a full-employment level of income is sharply defined is the model that denies the existence of any trade-off and that embodies a "natural rate" of unemployment, which cannot be permanently modified by shifts in the rate of aggregate spending.[7] If this model should, in fact, describe empirical reality, while, at the same time, the "budget balance at full employment" norm is pursued, either in its pristine form or in some Phillips-curve variant, the avenue is opened for a regime of continuous budget deficits which would be wholly ineffective in achieving the macroeconomic objectives for which they are created.

To this point, we have ignored what is perhaps the most important limitation on the operation of the alternative budgetary rule, which calls for balance at full-employment income. This is the extreme vulnerability of the rule in a political setting where fiscal decisions are made, not by wise persons immune from constituency pressures, but by ordinary politicians who are responsive to demands of the voting public. The directional biases toward budgetary expansion and toward deficit financing that we have discussed in Chapter 7 are exaggerated under any attempt to apply the alternative rule for budgetary management. The predictions made about the employment-increasing potential of budget deficits are likely to be unduly unrealistic on the optimistic side, while, at the same time, the inflation-producing results of these deficits are likely to be discounted. The targeted combinations of unemployment and inflation rates that emerge from the choices of politi-

6. In an argument related to our point here, Lucas has cast doubt upon the ability to use the parameters of econometric models for evaluating alternative public policies. The reason is that the selection of a policy will itself modify the actions of economic agents, thereby altering the behavior implied by the estimated parameters and vitiating the conclusions of the econometric model. See Robert E. Lucas, Jr., "Econometric Policy Evaluation: A Critique," in Karl Brunner and Allan H. Meltzer, eds., *The Phillips Curve and Labor Markets* (Amsterdam: North-Holland, 1976), pp. 19–46.

7. For a discussion, see Milton Friedman, "The Role of Monetary Policy," *American Economic Review* 58 (March 1968): 1–17.

cians are quite likely to lie off of the short-run Phillips curve for the economy rather than on it. Even if a point is selected that lies on the relevant curve, the relative weight given to the employment objective is likely to be high relative to that accorded to monetary stability.

Quite apart from biases in the selection of targets, however, the proposed rule is politically open to abuse because of the absence of any feedback constraint on error stemming from overoptimistic projections. Both the annually balanced budget and the balanced budget over the cycle contain some benchmarks that make it possible for citizens and politicians to judge whether the stated principle is being adhered to or being violated. Error becomes visible for all to see. No such possibility exists with the modern fiscal norm— "budget balance at full employment." There simply is no way that actual budgetary performance can be evaluated with a view to determine whether the rule is or is not being followed. A large current deficit can quite readily be passed off as actually reflecting a restrictive fiscal policy. And there is no way that this allegation can be tested, because the idealized conditions that would be required for a test will never exist, and could never exist.

The Budget Reform Act of 1974

The Congressional Budget and Impoundment Control Act of 1974 has been described by *U.S. News & World Report* as "a revolutionary budget reform intended to give Congress a tighter grip on the nation's purse strings. . . ." The passage of this act indicates that the elements of the Keynesian modification of our fiscal constitution have not gone wholly unrecognized. Such recognition that some things are awry with our fiscal conduct is an essential prerequisite to reversing the tendencies of the past generation. The act itself, however, is unlikely to be the revolutionary reform that *U.S. News & World Report* suggested.

The Budget Reform Act emerged from a recognition that previous budgetary procedures generated a bias toward spending and budget deficits. The total amount of spending emerged as the product of many individual appropriations decisions. No decision was ever made as to the total amount of public expenditure. Moreover, decisions regarding taxation were made independently of decisions regarding expenditure. A decision to increase expenditure could be made in isolation from decisions about whether that expenditure should be financed by increased taxation, by issuance of public debt, or by reduced expenditure for other services. It increasingly came to be recognized that such institutional practices created biases toward public spending and budget deficits.

This growing recognition inspired and informed the Budget Reform Act of 1974.[8] A Budget Committee was created for each house, and these committees were given the task of setting overall targets for revenues, expenditures, and the resulting deficit or surplus. As well as setting a target for the overall level of expenditure, these committees were supposed to apportion this amount among sixteen functional categories of public expenditure. A Congressional Budget Office was created to assist in this process, as well as to make five-year projections. These projections were designed to help gauge the future impact of present decisions. Under the previous setting for budgetary choice, programs would often be created with small initial expenditure requirements, but would soon undergo an explosive growth in spending requirements.

The fiscal year was changed to start on 1 October, rather than on 1 July. Accordingly, fiscal 1977 began on 1 October 1976, instead of 1 July 1976, as it would have done previously. By 15 May preceding the start of the new fiscal year, Congress is required to have passed its first concurrent resolution. This resolution contains tentative targets for outlays and revenues, as well as for such residually determined magnitudes as the budget deficit or surplus and the amount of national debt. Furthermore, this target amount for total outlay is apportioned among the sixteen functional categories. After the passage of this first concurrent resolution, the former congressional procedures take effect. Separate committees examined the various proposals for appropriations and revenues, with these various examinations being conducted in light of the first concurrent resolution. By late September, Congress is required to have passed the second concurrent resolution, with the fiscal year then start-

---

8. For a description and discussion of the act, see Committee for Economic Development, *The New Congressional Budget Process and the Economy* (New York: Committee for Economic Development, 1975); and Jesse Burkhead and Charles Knerr, "Congressional Budget Reform: New Decision Structures" (Paper presented at a conference, "Federal Fiscal Responsibility," March 1976), to be published in a volume of proceedings.

ing on 1 October. This second resolution is supposed to resolve any discrepancies that arise between the first resolution and the decisions that were made subsequently.

The Budget Reform Act is not the first attempt at instituting a comprehensive process of budget review. The Legislative Reorganization Act of 1946 also attempted to impose a congressional assessment of the entire budget. That legislation established a joint committee of the Senate and House that would determine an appropriation ceiling, the intention being that this ceiling would control the growth in expenditure. Only in 1949, however, did Congress manage to establish such a ceiling. And it promptly ignored that ceiling by approving appropriations that exceeded the ceiling by more than $6 billion. Until 1974, there were no further attempts at overall congressional control of the budget.

It is, of course, always possible that the 1974 act will prove to be more successful than the 1946 act. The act itself, however, does nothing to curb deficit spending. Rather, it merely requires that the projected level of the deficit be made explicit.[9] Moreover, any divergence of the second concurrent resolution from the first is likely to be in the direction of larger spending and larger deficits. It is unlikely indeed that the appropriations committees would generate projected outlays below the targets set in the first concurrent resolution. Any discrepancies would almost certainly be in the direction of increased appropriations. It is also unlikely that the second concurrent resolution would simply disallow all of these resulting discrepancies. While some may be disallowed, the second resolution is also likely to set higher expenditure levels, along with larger deficits. The most reasonable assessment of the Budget Reform Act seems to be, as Lenin might have put it: "Expenditure ceilings, like pie crusts, are meant to be broken."

Short-Term Politics for Long-Term Objectives

Since the Keynesian destruction of the balanced-budget principle, we have witnessed a parade of alternative principles, all pretending to function as con-

9. Some economists have suggested that the Keynesian-oriented staff of the Congressional Budget Office, created under the 1974 act, may exert a direct influence toward larger deficits rather than toward smaller. Comments by Beryl Sprinkel to this effect were reported in the *Washington Post,* 5 May 1976, p. D9.

straints on budgetary excesses. To date, none of these alternatives have been successful in this regard. Budgets continually become ever more bloated, and we have now become accustomed to thinking of a 2- or 3-percent inflation as an objective we might possibly attain once again in the dim future. One now hears little about price stability, and the pace of the extension of bureaucratic controls is still quickening.

The complex rules and principles that have been advanced over the past generation have given an illusion of control. They appear to mitigate the apparent disparity between common-sense notions of responsible fiscal behavior and the widely sensed irresponsibility of present budgetary outcomes. These complex rules suggest that the appearance of irresponsibility is illusory, and that such observed budgetary behavior is really necessary to fulfill the precepts of fiscal responsibility. These arguments say we must travel the deficits road to surplus (or balance). Since our political conversion to Keynesianism during the Kennedy administration, we have been told that deficits today will stimulate the economy into producing full-employment surpluses tomorrow. Only tomorrow never seems to come. Deficits have become ever more firmly ensconced as a way of life, and the imminency of surpluses has receded—once we were told that it would take only a few years before the federal budget would be in surplus, but the number of years lengthens as the size of the deficits grows. Can any honest person realistically predict balance in the federal budget?[10]

Such complex budgetary rules as "balance at full employment" serve to rationalize budgetary irresponsibility by playing upon the sense that the present is unique and involves special circumstances, and that once these circumstances have been dealt with, we can revert to the rules applicable to "normal" settings. This is like the alcoholic who has some sense that all is not well with his conduct of his life, and who resolves to get hold of himself once the

---

10. The conventional journalistic wisdom on economists' views on budget balance was expressed in *Time*'s report on the economic advisers to the 1976 presidential contenders. The account stated that "Martin Anderson is one of the few economists who still believe that a literally balanced federal budget is possible" (*Time*, 26 April 1976, p. 54). While we should acknowledge that relatively few of our professional colleagues would now believe that budget balance is *desirable*, we should indeed be surprised to learn that few consider balance to be *possible*, unless, of course, the political constraints that we emphasize are incorporated into the prediction.

particular tensions he currently finds unbearable have passed him by. Only each day, week, or month presents a fresh set of tensions, unusual circumstances, and special conditions, so "normalcy" never returns, for either the alcoholic or the Keynesian political economy.

We have been witnessing the political working out of a conflict familiar to all of us, that between short-term and long-term considerations. We all recognize that the fixation on some long-term objective or goal is necessary to provide a disciplinary base for judging short-term choices. But if that long-term objective is not fixed in mind, or if it is permitted to be swamped by momentary, short-term considerations, the result almost surely will produce a drift in directions far removed from those that would be considered desirable.

Politicians themselves have, for the most part, short time horizons. For most of them, each election presents a critical point, and the primary problem they face is getting past this hurdle. "Tis better to run away today to be around to fight again another day" might well be the motto. This is not to say that politicians never look beyond the next election in choosing courses of action, but only that such short-term considerations dominate the actions of most of them. Such features are, of course, an inherent and necessary attribute of a democracy. But when this necessary attribute is mixed with a fiscal constitution that does not restrain the ordinary spending and deficit-creating proclivities, the result portends disaster.

We do not suggest that we relinquish political and public control of our affairs, but only that politicians be placed once again in an effective constitutional framework in which budgetary manipulation for purposes of enhancing short-run political survival is more tightly restrained, thereby giving fuller scope to the working of the long-term forces that are so necessary for the smooth functioning of our economic order. Just as an alcoholic might embrace Alcoholics Anonymous, so might a nation drunk on deficits and gorged with government embrace a balanced budget and monetary stability.

11. What about Full Employment?

Introduction

Much of our argument in this book may find widespread acceptance. But many who find our diagnosis persuasive may reject our implicit prescription of a return to the old-fashioned norms of fiscal conduct. The fiscal policy clock cannot simply be turned back, and, since the Employment Act of 1946, the United States has been committed to pursuing policies that promote full employment. Those who accept our diagnosis but who balk at our implied remedy are likely to ask, "What about full employment?" The old-fashioned medicine might have been fine for the pre-Keynesian era, but the complex economic and political setting of the modern world may seem to dictate the administration of more potent Keynesian-like elixir. Can we really do other than pursue activist fiscal policies until the economy gets on and stays on its potential growth path? Perhaps then, and only then, we might return to something resembling the rules.

Current Unemployment
and the Quandary of Policy

With the passage of the Employment Act of 1946, Congress declared that it was the

> policy and responsibility of the Federal Government . . . to coordinate and utilize all its plans, functions, and resources for the purpose of creating and maintaining . . . conditions under which there will be afforded useful employment for those able, willing, and seeking to work.

The Council of Economic Advisers was created to assist in the implementation of this act. Just what constitutes "full employment" was not defined in the act, and, moreover, it is an inherently unobservable variable.

Despite this necessary imprecision in definition, the Employment Act is exceedingly significant, for with its enactment, the Congress sanctified the principal thrust of the Keynesian analysis. By implication, the free enterprise economy was officially conceived to be unstable; it became the task of government to act as a balance wheel to promote stability and growth. The Employment Act mandated that the government practice compensatory policy so as to promote full employment. Whenever employment declined below that level defined to be "full employment," government seemed legally to be required to undertake expansive budgetary and/or monetary policy.[1]

But what is full employment? The Keynesian economists have never been precisely clear on this question, and their acceptable targets have been moved progressively downward through time. In the 1962 Report of the Council of Economic Advisers, full employment was officially defined to be present when there was a 4-percent measured rate of unemployment.[2] This was, however, taken to be only some interim rate, with the long-run objective rate considerably lower. The much-discussed Humphrey-Hawkins bill in 1976 set out a 3-percent target rate, to be attained within four years. Historically, however, unemployment in the United States has only infrequently, and then only temporarily, fallen below 4 percent. During the sixty-three-year period after the creation of the Federal Reserve System, the period 1913–1975, there were only twenty years in which unemployment averaged 4 percent or less. Ten of

1. The concluding clause of the paragraph in which the citation in the text appears goes, "and to promote maximum employment, production, and purchasing power." This wording suggests that the commitment to full employment is not absolute, and the discussion of the trade-off between unemployment and inflation that surfaced in the late 1950s was a response to this perceived ambiguity. What this meant in practice was that full employment was only a relatively absolute absolute.

2. *Economic Report of the President, 1962*, p. 46. "Okun's Law," which was developed to give a quantitative estimate of the loss from unemployment, is based on this 4-percent measure, for its measure of the loss from unemployment is

$$L = 3(U - .04)GNP,$$

where U is the rate of unemployment and GNP is the dollar value of Gross National Product. See Arthur Okun, "The Gap between Actual and Potential Output," in Arthur Okun, ed., *The Battle against Unemployment* (New York: Norton, 1965), pp. 13–22.

these years—1918, 1943–1945, 1951–1953, and 1966–1968—occurred during periods when the United States was at war, although the mobilization was not so intense in the latter two periods as it was in the former two. The normal rate of unemployment, though unmeasurable, would appear to lie somewhat above 4 percent. During the fifteen-year period 1946–1960, a period that included both moderate mobilization and moderate recession, as well as predating the full Keynesian conversion of our politicians, unemployment averaged 4.5 percent. Even if we could make the heroic assumption that the institutional-structural features affecting employment have remained invariant over the long periods noted, it would seem clear that the "normal" rate of unemployment lies considerably above 4 percent. And, of course, it would be illegitimate to make such an assumption of invariance through time. Both demographic shifts within the labor force (toward younger and female workers) and policy changes (unemployment compensation, extended minimum wage coverage, increases in welfare payments and retirement support) have had the effect of increasing the level of unemployment that would be consistent with any specified rate of inflation.[3]

A national economic policy targeted to achieve, say, a 4-percent rate of unemployment is likely to be inflationary on the one hand and unattainable on the other, especially in the long run, at least in the absence of corrective policies aimed at structural features of labor markets. Efforts to attain such a rate of measured unemployment would probably generate increasing rates of inflation, with little demonstrable effects on employment itself.[4]

Since 1964, when we entered the Great Society stage of our national history, we have lived through a period in which federal budget deficits have been increasing rapidly, along with explosive growth in the size of government. In the early years of this period, 1964–1969, unemployment fell steadily, along with continuing inflation. Taken alone, this mid-1960s experience

---

3. For a brief general discussion, see Michael L. Wachter, "Some Problems in Wage Stabilization," *American Economic Review* 66 (May 1976): 65–66. For a specific analysis of unemployment compensation, see Martin Feldstein, "Unemployment Compensation: Adverse Incentives and Distribution Anomalies," *National Tax Journal* 17 (June 1974): 231–244.

4. Michael L. Wachter estimated that the rate of unemployment consistent with price-level stability was 5.5 percent in 1975, which he admitted to be a minimal figure. See Wachter, pp. 66–67.

might suggest a changing trade-off between inflation and unemployment. But economic life is not so simple. Inflation may reduce unemployment for a time, but it also distorts the structure of the economy in the process. Such structural distortions may, in turn, require an increase in unemployment before the economy can make the readjustments that are necessary to dissipate the distortions. This day of reckoning can be postponed only through ever-increasing inflation, or through the replacement of the free economy by a command economy, one in which direct controls are imposed. In the years after 1969, unemployment increased along with inflation, and the accelerated unemployment experienced in the recession of 1974–1975 attests to the difficulty of slowing down a rate of inflation once started.

The combination of substantial unemployment and inflation creates a quandary for economic policy. The Employment Act of 1946 seems to commit the nation to public policies designed to promote full employment. In the simplistic Keynesian theory of economic process (and the Employment Act implied an acceptance of this Keynesian theory), total employment varies directly with the volume of total spending. The mere presence of unemployment provides a signal for expansionary policies that increase aggregate or total spending in the economy. Inflation, by contrast, can be alleviated only through contractionary policies that reduce aggregate spending. Unemployment calls for expansion, while inflation calls for contraction. This is the quandary, pure and simple.

The Keynesian Theory of Employment

It will be useful again to summarize the basic Keynesian theory of economic policy that allegedly supports the politically dominant policy paradigm. If some such *extraordinary* and exogenous force or event, a collapse of the banking-monetary structure, a revaluation of the national currency at some disequilibrium level, or a major physical catastrophe, has generated a reduction in the aggregate demand for goods and services in the economy, a reduction that has dramatically modified business expectations, output and employment will have been reduced, possibly along with prices and wages, although the latter response may lag behind the former. In this setting, an explicit program of expanding aggregate spending in the economy through fiscal measures (the efficacy of monetary policy may be temporarily reduced by the existence of excess liquidity) will modify business expectations and will succeed in expanding the total volume of spending relative to total labor costs (and, to employers, this will amount to a reduction in real wages as a share of product prices). As a result, output and employment will expand, possibly along with some increase in prices, although the latter may again lag behind the former.

This summarizes our understanding of the theory of macroeconomic policy, as presented by Keynes himself, with the one exception that he falsely proclaimed it to be a *general theory*, presumably applicable to economic environments in which no extraordinary event has occurred at all, environments that are not remotely akin to those of the depressed 1930s. It seems quite likely that Keynes, always willing to change his mind, would have quickly abandoned these claims to generality had he lived into the years following World War II. But his followers, the Keynesians who became his disciples charged with spreading the gospel, made a simplistic extension of the basic model to economic environments for which the whole "theory" is clearly inapplicable.

If, instead of some extraordinary and exogenous event that has literally plunged the economy into a depressed state, financially and psychologically, endogenous structural features of the market (including governmentally enforced regulations and restrictions) have generated a level of unemployment (say, 5, 6, 7, or even 8 percent) that is deemed "unacceptable" against some arbitrarily chosen standard (with, say, a 3-percent or a 4-percent target), the policy norm derived from the Keynesian model may not be at all appropriate. In such a setting, the Keynesians would have us apply essentially the same expansionary tools as those applied in the extraordinarily depressed economy. Aggregate spending "should" be expanded so as to increase the level of employment. And, as we have noted, the Keynesians did succeed in convincing the politicians to this effect.

When this falsely applied theory of policy is appended to an apparent legislative mandate for the achievement of "full employment," a mandate that was, itself, a product of depression mentality, the policy prescriptions become straightforward. When unemployment exists, for any reason, the stream of spending must be increased. Conversely, any policy that reduces aggregate spending must increase unemployment. Unfortunately, this states all too perfectly the macroeconomic policy paradigm of modern democracy. Any politicians who want to appear responsive to the needs of the unemployed must support expansionary fiscal measures.[5] (The parade of presidential hopefuls in 1976 who mouthed the simplest of Keynesian propositions should, in itself, offer substantive proof for the central argument of this book.) Only some misanthropic capitalist or his lackey would suggest that the unemployment observed in the 1970s may not be much reduced by further increases in total spending, that such reductions that could be achieved might be short-lived, and that these could be secured only at the expense of accelerated inflation. Herein lies what may properly be considered our national economic-political tragedy, one that finds its origins in ideas that were both imperfectly understood and inappropriately applied.[6] Having entered the realm of political discourse, however, these ideas cannot be readily exorcised by the empirical findings of the academic economists.

The Inflation-Unemployment Trade-off

In its early textbook formulations, although not in Keynes' own work, the Keynesian theory of macroeconomic management posited a categorical distinction between the conditions under which expansionary policies would be inflationary and the conditions under which they would generate noninflationary increases in employment and output. Up to a certain level of employment, expansionary policies would elicit increases in employment and output, but without increasing prices. Beyond that level of employment, expansionary policies would increase prices, but without increasing employment and output.

5. Werner Zohlnhöfer has developed a similar point in much more general terms. He argues that a politician or party in opposition to the ruling coalition can never enhance chances of success by lending support to anti-inflationary measures. See Werner Zohlnhöfer, "Eine politische Theorie der schleichenden Inflation," in *Schriften des Vereins für Socialpolitik, Gesellschaft für Wirtschafts- und Sozialwissenschaft*, N. F. Band 85/1 (1975), pp. 533–555.

6. By common argument, the situation in Great Britain in the late 1970s was even worse than that in the United States. For a set of assessments in 1976, see John Flemming et al., *Catch 76*, Occasional Paper no. 47 (London: Institute of Economic Affairs, 1976). Also, see Peter Jay, *Employment, Inflation, and Politics*, Occasional Paper no. 46 (London: Institute of Economic Affairs, 1976).

It was always recognized that this view was but a simplified representation, though one that captured adequately the central features of the phenomena under examination. By the late 1950s, this simplistic view gave way to the widespread realization that acceptably full employment and stability in the value of money might be inconsistent. In an economy with strong labor unions and/or governmental wage floors, both full employment and a stable price level were not likely to be achieved; some trade-off was necessary. If unemployment was to be reduced to tolerable levels, increasing prices might have to be tolerated. The empirical basis of this trade-off was the so-called "Phillips curve," and the inflation-unemployment relationship became the focal point of almost all discussions of macroeconomic policy after the late 1950s.[7] Inflation and unemployment became matters of political choice, and a politician who assigned weight to stability in the purchasing power of money was automatically branded by popular opinion as someone who favored higher rates of unemployment, as someone who would deliberately create food-stamp lines.

Like the simplistic Keynesian theory of employment, the inflation-unemployment trade-off possessed a striking attention-arresting power. This trade-off came to dominate the images people formed as to the nature of reality, and democratic politics conformed to this image. When this is combined with the view that inflation is a problem not nearly so severe as unemployment, the inflationary bias becomes transparent. What decent politician could countenance greater unemployment simply to attain price-level stability?

By the late 1960s, the foundations of the inflation-unemployment trade-off began to erode, in the minds of academicians, though not in the minds of citizens and politicians. The Phillips curve, it came to be realized, de-

---

7. As noted earlier, the basic paper is A. W. Phillips, "The Relation between Unemployment and the Rate of Change of Money Wages in the United Kingdom, 1861–1957," *Economica* 25 (November 1958): 283–299. In this article, the trade-off was between wage inflation and unemployment. This relation was subsequently transformed into the more familiar relation between price inflation and unemployment. The American discussion was inaugurated by the famous Samuelson-Solow paper. See Paul A. Samuelson and Robert M. Solow, "Analytical Aspects of Anti-Inflation Policy," *American Economic Review* 50 (May 1960): 177–194.

scribed only a short-run, not a long-run, trade-off.[8] Expansions in aggregate demand, accompanied by some inflation, could reduce unemployment in the short run, but only because the inflationary effects were not fully anticipated. Once the predictable effects of inflation on real wages came to be understood, permanent structural features of the economy would reassert themselves. As expectations came to be adjusted to inflation, unemployment would rise to roughly the level determined by these structural features. The price level would, of course, be higher because of the expanded monetary spending, but there would be no permanent increase in employment. A permanent increase in prices would be the cost of, at best, a temporary and short-lived reduction in unemployment.

The idea that the inflation-unemployment trade-off can be exploited only in the short run, not in the long run, embodies the notion of a "natural rate" of employment. This natural rate of unemployment corresponds to full employment in the classical, non-Keynesian analytical framework.[9] Unemployment can be reduced below this natural rate only by a continually accelerating inflation. If, for instance, a 4-percent rate of unemployment is accepted as an objective of macroeconomic policy, and if the natural rate of unemployment lies above 4 percent, say in the vicinity of 5 percent, pursuit of the standard policies of Keynesian management will produce a continually accelerating inflation in pursuit of this unattainable objective.

The Inflation-Unemployment Spiral

This has come increasingly to be recognized by economists, and much of the earlier academic support for expansionary fiscal-monetary policies based on the alleged Phillips-curve trade-off has disappeared. Politically, however, the arguments proceed unchecked, and it seems highly unlikely that elected politicians can adhere to the discipline that would be required to escape from the inflationary spiral. The experience with the recession of 1974–1975 offered a test.

8. A survey of alternative perspectives toward the Phillips curve is presented in Thomas M. Humphrey, "Changing Views of the Phillips Curve," *Federal Reserve Bank of Richmond, Monthly Review* 59 (July 1973): 2–13.

9. See, for instance, Milton Friedman, "The Role of Monetary Policy," *American Economic Review* 58 (May 1968): 1–17.

Why was the American economy characterized by "stagflation" in 1974 and 1975? Unemployment seemed clearly to be above any plausible "natural rate," while, at the same time, the price level continued to rise. There are two complementary parts of an explanation for this phenomenon. The double-digit inflation set off by the fiscal-monetary excesses of 1972 and 1973 set in motion fears of explosive hyperinflation; this caused the monetary authorities to decelerate the rate of monetary expansion. But, because of built-in expectations of the public concerning the continuance of accelerating rates of inflation, any deceleration in the rate of monetary expansion had an effect essentially the same as an actual reduction in aggregate demand would produce in a setting of monetary stability. The responses of business firms and consumers brought about reductions in output and employment, though upward pressures on prices were maintained, both because of lagged effects and because the deceleration was still within a range that allowed for continued inflation. Unemployment moved upward to levels that were probably well above the sustainable natural rate, given the structural features of the United States' economy.

"Stagflation" could, therefore, be explained in this way, even if we should leave out of account the internal allocative distortions that long-continued inflation itself produced or might have produced. Once we allow for such distortions, any attempt to decelerate the rate of monetary expansion will generate more pronounced output and employment responses, with the magnitude of these being related directly to the length of the inflationary period. It is this second part of the overall explanation of "stagflation" that gives rise to the view that continued inflation, in itself, must be a direct cause of greater unemployment in any future period when any deceleration in the rate of inflation takes place.

Inflation has two effects. One effect is to lower real wages; this was Keynes' thesis, and it is this effect that is recognized by those who argue that, once inflation is fully anticipated, the rate of unemployment cannot be permanently reduced below its natural level. This effect gives the customary result of a short-run trade-off between inflation and unemployment, while any such trade-off is absent in the long run.

The other effect is a possible general disruption of the working of the market economy, reflected in the reallocations of resources that take place in response to the inflation-caused short-run shifts in relative prices, as well as in the reallocations that result in response to the increase in the rate of mistakes owing to the increased difficulty of rational economic calculation. As these allocative distortions become more important, a policy shift away from accelerating inflation both will generate a temporary increase in unemployment above the natural rate and will alter the length of time required to return to the natural rate. If the economy is to "recover" from the Keynesian-inspired inflationary spree, the recovery phase will necessarily involve unemployment above the natural rate, and this phase can be regarded as the "price" of the mistakes of the past.

Suppose, however, that a government necessarily subject to Keynesian pressures, and faced with an observed rise in unemployment above what seems to be the natural rate, does not carry through its anti-inflation commitment and decides instead to stimulate aggregate demand once again. This stimulatory policy unleashes two opposing forces. The temporary fall in the real-wage rate may reduce unemployment somewhat. But the removal of the allocative distortions is postponed and still further distortions are encouraged, which will, in turn, make a subsequent policy of retaining monetary stability more difficult.

If, on the other hand, an anti-inflation policy is carried through, and a rate of unemployment in excess of the natural rate is tolerated for a sufficient time, the economy will eventually "recover" in the sense that the rate of unemployment consistent with basic structural features will be attained. But if the day of reckoning is postponed through periodic injections of Keynesian stimulation, an inflation-unemployment spiral can develop. New doses of inflation may initially stimulate employment, but they will also increase the volume of mistaken, unsustainable economic decisions. The misallocations that stem from such errors will, in turn, generate reallocative unemployment. Should the economy be shocked with still a further dose of Keynesian expansionary medicine rather than being permitted gradually to adjust to its natural equilibrium, some short-run reduction in unemployment may take place once again. But additional mistakes, resource misallocations, will be again injected into the economy, and the rectification of these mistakes will, in turn, generate additional unemployment. In this way, a spiral of inflation and unemployment can result from Keynesian prescriptions. Inflation creates allocative mistakes, and these mistakes cannot be rectified costlessly. There are readjustment costs that simply must be borne before the economy can return to normal.[10] The day of reckoning can only be postponed, not for-given, and the longer it is postponed, the more frightful the eventual day of reckoning becomes.

Biting the Bullet

A policy of attempting to reduce unemployment through the stimulation of aggregate demand is shortsighted in a situation that is not structurally abnormal (such as the 1930s). Unemployment may be reduced temporarily, but the inflation will exacerbate the maladjustments contained within the economy. There is no costless cure for a maladjusted economy. Reallocations of capital and labor must take place before the economy's structure of production will once again reflect the underlying data to which a free economy adapts. The mistakes that result from people responding to the false signals generated by inflation must be worked out before the economy can return fully to normalcy. Recession is an inherent part of the recovery process; it is the economic analogue to a hangover for a nation that is drunk from Keynesian stimulation.

To attempt to maintain "full employment" is an act of delusion. The readjustments can be postponed, though with ever-increasing difficulty, but they cannot be prevented, at least within the context of a free society. The inflation-unemployment spiral that results from shortsighted efforts at demand stimulation will simply increase the dissonance between people's aspirations and their realizations. As a result, democratic institutions become more fragile. In Britain in the late 1970s, where the policy dilemma has been even more severe than that of the United States, there has been widespread discussion of the prospects of calling in some "leader," empowered to deal effectively with the issues, reflecting a yearning that emerges when people lose their faith in the ability of ordinary democratic process to produce meaningful patterns of economic and social existence.

---

10. A clear, early presentation of this theme can be found in Friedrich A. Hayek, *Prices and Production,* 2d ed. (London: Routledge and Kegan Paul, 1935). A general exposition is contained in Gottfried Haberler, *Prosperity and Depression,* 5th ed. (London: Allen & Unwin, 1964), pp. 29–72. A recent, formal development of this possibility occurs in Robert E. Lucas, Jr., "An Equilibrium Model of the Business Cycle," *Journal of Political Economy* 83 (December 1975): 1135–1137.

The Employment Act of 1946, one of our legacies from Lord Keynes, may come to be regarded as one of the more destructive pieces of legislation in our national history. This act pledges the government to do something it cannot possibly do, at least so long as our underlying fiscal and monetary institutions are themselves the primary source of instability. And if fiscal and monetary sources of instability were removed, there should be no need for an Employment Act. The political system is burdened with claims on which it cannot possibly deliver, at least within the context of a nonregimented society. The act has an inflationary bias, a bias that, as Joseph Schumpeter noted with remarkable perceptiveness and frightening prescience, can ultimately topple a liberal, democratic civil order.

So, What about Full Employment?

Our response to the query with which we opened this chapter must necessarily be a seemingly elusive one, for the mind-set within which this question would be posed to us is one that has been molded by the legacy of Lord Keynes. Discussion has been unduly concentrated on the end-result objective of employment, to the neglect of the processes within which end results are produced.[11] Involuntary unemployment is indeed undesirable, but we must try to understand the institutional processes that may have produced an observed result before we act on the end result itself. It is a false vision of reality to infer that the selfsame processes are always at work, that involuntary employment necessarily reflects deficiency in aggregate demand.

In a competitive market system of economic organization, there will, of course, be instances of observed involuntary unemployment. This unemployment will result from such factors as shifts in consumer preferences, the development of new technologies, and errors made by businesses and consumers. Insofar as elements of the economy are noncompetitive, observed instances of involuntary unemployment may be more widespread. Job search becomes more difficult as more areas are closed by restrictions on entry.

---

11. Many of the strictures against end-state norms of justice raised by Robert Nozick might readily be translated into strictures against the policy-oriented discussion of "full employment" in the post-Keynesian period. See Robert Nozick, *Anarchy, State, and Utopia* (New York: Basic Books, 1974).

Nonetheless, all such instances of involuntary unemployment will tend to be, first of all, of short duration, and they would tend to occur fairly *evenly* over time. The *concentration* or bunching required to produce what might be considered an economywide recession or depression is a quite different phenomenon, and must be explained by economywide causes. In the Great Depression of the 1930s, the involuntary unemployment did result from a deficiency in aggregate demand, produced largely if not totally by the failure of governments to maintain a stable monetary-fiscal framework.[12] The Keynesian emphasis tended to neglect the more general institutional or framework features, which allow us to make a conceptually distinct separation between the legitimate responsibility of government to maintain a stable monetary-fiscal framework and the sometimes expedient extensions of government activity beyond such limits, extensions that tend, in themselves, to be a source of instability.

Our answer to the query in the chapter title, then, must be a roundabout one. Full employment should not, indeed cannot, be promoted directly through government policies of aggregate demand management. Such policies merely compound past mistakes with present mistakes, thereby making the economy perform ever more poorly. Full employment can be promoted only through a regime in which government conducts its affairs in a manner that avoids injecting new sources of instability into the economy. We shall examine these constitutional principles for stability in the next chapter.

---

12. See the careful and thorough documentation of this point in Milton Friedman and Anna J. Schwartz, *A Monetary History of the United States, 1867–1960* (Princeton: Princeton University Press, 1963), pp. 299–419.

12. A Return to Fiscal Principle

The Thrill Is Gone

Our principal emphasis in this book is on history, analysis, and diagnosis, three separate but related elements in a critical interpretation of the Keynesian legacy. Our post-Keynesian economic order has not performed as promised. This seems clear as diagnosis, and diagnosis is our main task in this book. We do not conceive our own role as "saviors," and we do not consider ourselves obliged to preach some new "religion" to those who must, directly or indirectly, make economic-political policy choices. There may exist several ways to "recover" adequately from the deficit-ridden, inflation-prone policy pattern that seems inherent in the workings of ordinary democratic process as they are presently constituted. At best, therefore, any proposal that we advance in this final chapter should be treated as only one among several possible alternatives.

Perhaps the most sanguine stance, and one that is probably held by some of those who still would classify themselves as truly "Keynesian," embodies the faith that practicing politicians and, by implication, their voting constituencies will begin to behave "responsibly." Holders of this view tend to believe that, once politicians come to understand the long-term results of short-term policy errors, they will start behaving like economic statesmen. This roseate projection of a modified political and public behavior, without basic structural or institutional change, would, if it came true, refute the central thesis of this book. Such a refutation would indeed be welcome, and we should, quite willingly, relegate this book to the dustbin of anachrony, happy in our newfound knowledge that things were not really so bad as they seemed to us in 1976, when this book was written.

An almost equally hopeful outlook, and one that would also partially if not wholly refute our arguments, embodies the conviction that the required structural-institutional reforms have been taken, that the Budget Reform Act of 1974, when viewed from the vantage point of hindsight in, say, 1990, will be seen as having worked miracles. Our own analysis suggests that the reforms reflected in this particular legislation are not those required for the democratic political process to rid itself of the fundamental biases left from the Keynesian legacy. The reforms promised by the 1974 budget legislation are aimed at a set of flaws in budget making that are quite different from those we have examined here. This legislation aims to correct those problems stemming from the piecemeal consideration by Congress of the federal government's budget. To the extent that the newly established committees and procedures are effective, Congress will come closer to considering the budget a normative unit subject to explicit choice, and not a result that emerges from the behavior of many noncoordinated revenue and expenditure committees. This step, in itself, well may act to increase the overall responsibility in budgetary decision making.

But there is nothing in the 1974 legislation, or in its subsequent institutional changes, that imposes a norm for relating the two sides of the fiscal account, nothing that acts as a putative replacement for budget balance in the old-time or pre-Keynesian fiscal constitution. After 1976, if the intentions of the Budget Reform Act are to be followed, Congress will be somewhat more explicit in the creation of budget deficits. Such explicitness may reduce somewhat the size of the deficits, although the possibility that deficits could become larger cannot be ruled out. Regardless of particular direction, however, it seems beyond the limits of plausibility to suggest that explicitness alone will literally transform the behavior of modern politicians.

Nonetheless, this legislation, along with other observed events, surely attests to the verdict that the Keynesian allure is waning. The 1974 legislation was, in one sense, a direct response to the impoundment controversy that arose in the early 1970s, a controversy that called public attention to the explosive growth in federal spending and to the budget deficits that facilitated this growth. The constitutional issues raised during this controversy, although important in their own right, are not relevant here except insofar as the outcome tended to place upon Congress the charge to get its own house in order.

There are additional signs of a gradual awakening to the Keynesian dangers. In the summer of 1975, a Senate subcommittee held hearings on the possible desirability of a constitutional amendment that would require the federal government to balance its budget, except in times of declared national emergency. Such hearings would have been inconceivable in 1965. Members of the Democratic Research Organization of the House of Representatives commenced in early 1976 to consider alternative means of restoring fiscal responsibility.

The Case for Constitutional Norms

These various activities indicate a widening recognition of a developing fiscal-economic crisis, and the gradual acknowledgment by members of Congress that attempts must be made to put institutional halters on their own tendency to spend without taxing and, in consequence, to spend too much. The absence of an effective budgetary rule or norm, something against which budget making can be evaluated, is coming to be acutely sensed by those involved in it. The dwindling number of overt Keynesians to be found offer nothing other than the ultimately dangerous "budget balance at high employment" norm. This norm, which gives the appearance of promoting fiscal responsibility, seems almost ideally tailored to promote the opposite.

There are two quite distinct steps to be taken in moving toward genuinely effective fiscal reform. The first is that of recognizing explicitly that a meaningful constitutional norm is required, independently of just what this norm might be within rather broad limits. Budgets cannot be left adrift in the sea of democratic politics. They must be constructed within constraints that impose external form and coherence on the particular decisions about size and distribution which an annual budget reflects. The elected politicians, who must be responsive to their constituents, the governmental bureaucracy as well as the electorate, need something by way of an external and "superior" rule that will allow them to forestall the persistent demands for an increased flow of public-spending benefits along with reduced levels of taxation. Even those who might disagree most strongly with our favorable interpretation of the potential effectiveness of the rule for budget balance may acknowledge the necessity of some alternative rule that will constrain specific budget making within defined limits, a rule that is "constitutional" in this basic meaning of the term.

There are several qualities that any such rule must possess if it is to be effective. First of all, it must be relatively simple and straightforward, capable of being understood by members of the public. Highly sophisticated rules that might be fully understood only by an economists' priesthood can hardly qualify on this count alone. Secondly, an effective rule must be capable of offering clear criteria for adherence and for violation. Both the politicians and the public must be able readily to discern when the rule is being broken. Finally, and most importantly, the fiscal rule must reflect and express values held by the citizenry, for then adherence to the precepts of the rule may, to some extent, be regarded as sacrosanct. These three basic qualities add up to a requirement that any effective budgetary rule must be understood to "make sense" to the ordinary voter.

The Case for Budget Balance

It is in recognition of these qualities that we are led to a specific rule, the second step in any proposal for fiscal reform. We are led to propose an avowed reversal of the Keynesian destruction of budget balance, an outcome that would be accomplished through an explicit reestablishment of balance between the two sides of the fiscal account as the overriding constraint on public outlays. The principle of budget balance has the great advantage of simplicity. It was, is, and can be understood by everyone, and the translation of the principles for private financial responsibility to those for governments tends to facilitate such an understanding. Furthermore, and perhaps most importantly, despite the Keynesian conversion of our politicians, there remain significant residues of this norm in prevailing public attitudes, residues that can be brought to bear productively in any genuine restoration.

Given the fact of the Keynesian conversion, however, along with the observed political and public disrespect for the balanced-budget rule since the 1960s, there is little chance for reincarnation of the rule in some informal and unwritten, yet binding, element of our fiscal constitution. Precisely because we have allowed the Keynesian teachings to destroy the constraining influence of this part of our previously informal fiscal constitution, restoration must now involve something more formal, more specific, more explicitly confining than that which fell victim to the Keynesian onslaught. Restoration will require a constitutional rule that will become legally as well as morally binding, a rule that is explicitly written into the constitutional document of the United States.

It is on the basis of such considerations as these that we have supported, and continue to support, efforts to amend the United States Constitution so as to require the federal government to balance its budget, efforts which, as noted above, themselves suggest a growing awareness of the potentially disastrous Keynesian legacy.[1] Various versions of proposed amendments have been offered, almost all of which contain escape clauses that allow for departures from budget balance (presumably, to allow for budget deficits; little or no note is made of departures in the opposing direction) during periods of declared national emergencies. Political reality indicates to us that some such escape clause must be incorporated, but this, in itself, need not seriously inhibit the potential force of a budget-balance rule. The escape clauses proposed require that the Congress, in a separate resolution requiring perhaps two-thirds of each house, declare the existence of a national emergency, either war or economic distress. The centrally important element of the budget-balance rule, treated as a formal amendment to the Constitution, is that the Congress recognize it to be such, and that departures from the rule be acknowledged as departures from a standard that is itself independently existent and which remains invariant through time.

Fiscal Decisions under Budget Balance

It is perhaps as important to discuss what such a constitutional rule will not do as it is to discuss what it will do. Our emphasis has been on the constraining influence of such a rule, on its potential for eliminating the biased growth of the public sector of the economy and for reducing dramatically the sources of inflation. But too much should not be made of the constraints in any absolute sense. Nothing in a straightforward rule for budget balance dictates, and indeed nothing should so dictate, that total government spending be maintained at some predetermined level, either in absolute terms or relative

1. For a 1975 statement in support of these efforts, see James M. Buchanan and Richard E. Wagner, "Deficit Spending in Constitutional Perspective," in *Balancing the Budget*, Hearings before the Subcommittee on Constitutional Amendments, Committee of the Judiciary, United States Senate, 94th Congress, 1st Session, 23 September 1975 (Washington: U.S. Government Printing Office, 1975), pp. 61–64.

to national income. Decisions concerning the amount of resources to be allocated governmentally will be made through the ordinary political processes, with or without the existence of a rule for budget balance. The restoration of the balanced-budget rule will serve only to allow for a somewhat more conscious and careful weighting of benefits and costs. The rule will have the effect of bringing the real costs of public outlays to the awareness of decision makers; it will tend to dispel the illusory "something for nothing" aspects of fiscal choice.

Nor is there anything in a balanced-budget rule, as such, that influences the allocation of outlays within the overall budget. The mix between, say, defense and welfare may be explicitly defined either with or without a constraining rule requiring overall budget balance. And the introduction of such an external constraint should do nothing to tilt or bias the political process either toward more defense or toward more welfare spending.

Tax Rates and Spending Rates as Residual Budget Adjustors

A constitutional requirement that the federal government balance outlays with revenues, except in extraordinary times, well might remain unenforced and unenforceable if its language fails to specify means through which balance between the two sides of the fiscal account is to be maintained. What would happen if the budgeted outlays, approved by both the Congress and the president, should be projected to exceed (or to fall short of) tax receipts? It is relatively easy to think of situations in which a constitutional requirement for balance might exist without an adjustment mechanism, in which case budget deficits might continue to emerge, with little or no feedback effects on the decision-making process itself. (In this respect, the requirements might operate much as the legal limit on the size of the national debt.) In order to avoid this possibility, it seems necessary that any formal rule for budget balance include a specific adjustment mechanism, one that would be triggered automatically by an emergence of an outlay-revenue differential over and beyond some defined threshold. The adjustment should be automatic in the sense that it would be effectively immunized from current decision making; it should come into play through the operation of the rule itself.

As with the form of the rule itself, however, there are alternative ways of constructing the adjustment mechanism. Either rates of tax or rates of outlay may serve as the residual adjustors, or some combination of both might suffice. In this connection, we may recall an alleged "principle" in nineteenth-century public-finance theory. Individuals, so the principle goes, must adjust spending to income. Governments, by contrast, may adjust incomes (revenues) to spending requirements or "needs." Independently considered, this so-called "principle" is wholly fallacious because the concept of "requirements" or "needs" is as open-ended for governments as it is for private persons. But insofar as a difference exists, the implication is that, under a balanced-budget rule, tax rates "should" be the residual adjusting device. That is to say, if rates of outlay threaten to exceed rates of revenue collection, the emerging gap should trigger an automatic increase in tax rates, estimated to be sufficient to close the gap within defined threshold limits. This form of adjustment tends to bias the rule in favor of the public as opposed to the private sector; an impending budget deficit is reconciled by tax increases which reduce the demand for privately provided services.[2]

On the other hand, the constitutional rule might include adjustment in rates of outlay rather than in rates of tax. If prospective outlays, as budgeted, threaten to exceed revenue receipts by more than defined limits, this might require specific cutbacks in rates of outlay, with tax rates remaining invariant. Under this method of adjustment, the deficit is contained by spending reductions which will increase the demands for private market services. The choice between these two methods of adjustment can influence the allocation of resources between private and public sectors. While our preferred adjustment would involve rates of outlay rather than rates of tax, in part reflecting a reaffirmation that the principles of sound finance are essentially the same for governments and persons, the choice among adjustment mechanisms is insignificant relative to the establishment of an effective rule for budget balance per se.[3]

---

2. In the discussion prior to the enactment of the budget reform legislation of 1974, William Niskanen advanced a proposal that would have required that tax rates be automatically increased if Congress failed to keep spending within its own chosen target levels. See William Niskanen, *Structural Reform of the Federal Budget Process* (Washington: American Enterprise Institute, 1973).

3. For a general discussion of the residual adjustment in budgets, as these affect fiscal

If the residual adjustment is defined in rates of outlay, the simplest version would require across-the-board reductions in rates of spending on all budgetary components when the threshold of imbalance is exceeded. More complex variants of an automatic adjustment might insulate certain budgetary components as "untouchable" under the restrictions of the norm, while concentrating all of the possibly dictated outlay reductions on remaining components. (Something closely akin to this actually happens in state-local governments which act to postpone capital spending programs when faced with unexpected revenue shortfalls, while, at the same time, these units try to maintain more or less stable rates of operational spending.)[4]

A Specific Proposal

In the explicit acknowledgment that our proposal is only one among several possible alternatives that might be discussed, we should recommend that the Constitution of the United States be amended so as to include the following provisions:

1. The president shall be required to present annually to Congress a budget that projects federal outlays equivalent to federal revenues.
2. The Congress, both in its initial budgetary review, and in its subsequent approval, shall be required to act within the limits of a budget that projects federal outlays equivalent to federal revenues. (There is, of course, no requirement that the congressional budget be the same as that submitted by the president.)
3. In the event that projections prove in error, and a budget deficit beyond specified limits occurs, federal outlays shall be automatically adjusted

---

choices, see James M. Buchanan, *Public Finance in Democratic Process* (Chapel Hill: University of North Carolina Press, 1967), Chs. 7 and 8 especially.

4. One thing to be avoided in any variant of an automatic adjustment scheme would seem to be attempts to protect outlays on salaries for legislative and bureaucratic personnel. In fact, a strong case could be made for requiring disproportionate adjustment in this component of the federal budget, since this would provide an indirect means of encouraging compliance with the constitutional norm for maintaining overall balance in the fiscal account. It would be difficult to think of much legislative or bureaucratic agitation to exceed budget-balance guidelines if the penalties were known to include explicit reductions in governmental salaries.

downward to restore projected balance within a period of three months. If a budget surplus occurs, funds shall be utilized for retirement of national debt.

4. Provisions of this amendment shall be made fully effective within five years of its adoption. To achieve an orderly transition to full implementation, annual budget deficits shall be reduced by not less than 20 percent per year in each of the five years subsequent to the adoption of the amendment. Departure from this 20-percent rule for annual adjustment downward in the size of the deficit shall be treated in the same manner as departure from budget balance upon full implementation.

5. Provisions of this amendment may be waived only in times of national emergency, as declared by two-thirds of both houses of Congress, and approved by the president. Declarations of national emergency shall expire automatically after one year.

As an example, assume that the amendment proposed here is adopted in 1980, when the federal government's budget deficit is $100 billion on an annual basis. For 1981, the first year of the transition period, the deficit would have to be reduced to not more than $80 billion. If, in this first year, projected outlays exceed revenues by more than $80 billion, across-the-board reductions in all federal outlays would be required to attain this level of deficit.[5] Each subsequent year in the transition period of five years would be treated similarly, with the amendment becoming fully effective in 1985, from which time budget balance would be required rather than declining deficits. Requiring that the size of the deficit be reduced in each succeeding year of the transition period and that the deficit be wholly eliminated at the end of this period does not necessarily imply that federal spending programs in being at the time of the adoption of the amendment be curtailed or eliminated. The amendment proposed is aimed directly at controlling the size of the budget deficit, not at the absolute size of federal spending. To comply with the provisions of the proposed amendment, Congress may choose to increase tax rates or to reduce rates of growth in governmental outlays, or some combination of both. As noted earlier, the amendment will require only that the

5. Such an approach to restoring a balanced budget is also advocated in Raymond J. Saulnier, "Federal Spending, Budget Deficits, Inflation and Jobs," *Tax Review* 37 (June 1976): 21–24.

costs and benefits of public-spending programs be taken more explicitly into account.

Debt Retirement and Budget Surplus

As proposed, there is nothing in the constitutional rule that will allow for the accumulation of budgetary surpluses which might be utilized to amortize outstanding issues of national debt. Genuine return to the old-time fiscal religion would embody some attempt at reducing the amount of federal debt outstanding. This purpose may, however, be accomplished without the explicit creation of budgetary surpluses, simply by utilizing the parallel operations of the monetary authority, the Federal Reserve Board, in its role of providing new money for the economy as the economy grows. With a federal or national debt of the magnitude that exists (more than $700 billion in 1977), the monetary authority can use this resource as the means of increasing the monetary base for many years. In effect, the national debt would become monetized through time, and the annual budgetary burden of interest payments could be reduced gradually and finally eliminated.

To this point, we have said nothing specifically about the monetary "constitution." There is nothing about our constitutional proposals that would guarantee that the Federal Reserve Board would act responsibly to ensure that aggregate monetary stocks keep pace with the growth of real output in the economy. In the face of a constitutional amendment requiring budget balance, it seems highly improbable that the monetary decision makers would act as irresponsibly in this respect as they did in the tragic years of the 1930s. To guarantee against and to forestall such behavior, however, as well as to add still further predictability to the inclusive financial constitution, fiscal and monetary, we would support a supplementary constitutional amendment that would direct the Federal Reserve Board to increase the monetary base at a rate roughly equivalent to the rate of growth in real output in the national economy.[6] This supplementary monetary rule would have the effect of pro-

---

6. The complementary of rules for steady monetary growth and for a continually balanced budget, along with supporting argument for both, is developed in Robert E. Lucas, Jr., "An Equilibrium Model of the Business Cycle," *Journal of Political Economy* 83 (December 1975): 1113–1144.

moting approximate stability in the level of product prices. To the extent that real output should grow through time, the Federal Reserve Board, in following this monetary rule, would find it necessary to add to the monetary base. They could be directed to do this exclusively by the purchase and subsequent amortization of outstanding federal debt.[7]

In Summation

In several places and in several ways, our analysis should have made it clear that some set of fiscal principles must be restored; the Keynesian-inspired budgetary anarchy that we observe cannot continue. There are two complementary elements in our overall theme: One deals with the behavior of politicians and the other deals with the nature of our economic order.

Even if we accept the Keynesian story about the functioning of our economic order, democratic political pressures are likely to generate an asymmetrical application of the Keynesian prescriptions. For reasons that we explored in Part II, the Keynesian destruction of the balanced-budget constraint is likely to produce a bias toward budget deficits, monetary expansion, and public-sector growth. Politicians naturally want to spend and to avoid taxing. The elimination of the balanced-budget constraint enables politicians to give fuller expression to these quite natural sentiments.

If monetary changes were neutral in their impact on the economy, the inflationary bias of Keynesianism, in itself, would provide little reason for concern. But monetary changes are not neutral, for such changes affect the behavior of real variables within the economy. It is this nonneutrality of monetary changes that renders the Keynesianist inflationary bias so destructive. Money creation falsifies the signals that operate within the economy. In consequence, labor and capital move into employments where they cannot be sustained without increasing inflation. The false signals also reduce the informational content of such devices as standard accounting practices, thereby increasing the errors in decision making that are made by the participants in the economic process.

Politicians necessarily confront a tragic choice setting, for, being unable to

7. For a specific discussion of alternative monetary constitutions, see Leland B. Yeager, ed., *In Search of a Monetary Constitution* (Cambridge: Harvard University Press, 1962).

satisfy all desires, they must deny the desires of some. In the absence of a balanced-budget constraint, politicians can avoid confronting this setting directly. Since a decision to award benefits to some citizens must necessarily entail a decision to impose costs on others, is it so unreasonable to ask that this denial be made openly and honestly? Under such circumstances, a choice to approve spending that would benefit some citizens requires only that the politicians state openly just on whom it is that less will be spent, or just on whom it is that more taxes will be levied.

It might be objected that citizens have come to expect bread and circuses from their politicians. If their politicians do not provide such things, they will elect other politicians in their place. In view of such expectations, there are few politicians who would refuse to provide such bread and circuses. After all, is it not more pleasant to fulfill than to reject the desires of constituents? It is far more satisfying to give than to refuse, especially if it is not necessary to count the cost of giving. Who would not want to play Santa Claus? When a private citizen finds himself unable or unwilling to reject such desires, however, it is he who bears the cost of his actions. Politicians, however, act for the whole constituency. Their folly is our folly.

If a politician is forced by a balanced-budget constraint to reject various claimants, and loses office as a result, that may be regrettable, but no national harm is done. Should the politician be permitted to appease his normal gregariousness and avoid saying "no," however, the nation undermines both its prosperity and its liberty. A nation cannot survive with political institutions that do not face up squarely to the essential fact of scarcity: It is simply impossible to promise more to one person without reducing that which is promised to others. And it is not possible to increase consumption today, at least without an increase in saving, without having less consumption tomorrow. Scarcity is indeed a fact of life, and political institutions that do not confront this fact threaten the existence of a prosperous and free society.[8]

American prosperity and liberty were once the envy of the world, and the two went hand in hand. Our relative position in the national league tables

---

8. A widely acknowledged fact of political history is the increasing difficulty of dislodging incumbent members of Congress. This has often been attributed to the costs of entry and to similar financial barriers. Our argument suggests that a supplementary cause well may lie in the illusion that incumbent modern legislators do avoid facing up to scarcity constraints.

has been declining, a fact that cannot be disguised. Several countries in Western Europe have moved ahead of the United States in terms of measured income per head. Moreover, most Americans feel that individual liberty has been reduced. Regulations and controls have become ubiquitous, and, once installed, these seem impossible to remove or even to modify, despite widespread citizen complaint.

Although many other factors are surely present, some part of our difficulty can be blamed on the conversion to Keynesian ideas. A self-adjusting free economy, operating within a stable fiscal-monetary framework, lost its support, and we came to believe that only Keynesian management could ensure continued prosperity. The irony of our present situation is that the Keynesian fears may be coming true and, in the process, may be on the way to becoming part of a self-fulfilling prophecy.

We have suggested one set of proposals for fiscal and monetary reform, which, if enacted, would reverse the observed pattern. As noted, these are only one among several alternative sets that might be discussed. A first step in any such discussion is an understanding of the effects of Keynesianism on democratic political order. Only after such understanding can we begin to consider particular proposals for reform. In our view, a balanced budget would be one element in almost any acceptable constitutional framework. A democratic government is simply unable to act as a stabilizing force, and any attempts to force it to do so must ultimately be destabilizing.

There is simply no evidence at all that a free economy operating with a regime of fiscal-monetary stability is inherently unstable, or that such an economy must suffer excessive unemployment. There is accumulating evidence that an economy subject to attempted Keynesian management will be unstable, and that such management will itself produce unpredictable changes in employment. A few of the better textbooks of the 1970s have begun to relegate Keynesian economic theory to its appropriate place, as a model that partially explained the tragic events of a bizarre depression decade that is forty years in history. Surely it is time that the policy proposals derived from that theory also be displaced, along with the aging politicians whose time has also passed. The "Keynesian revolution" did take place; this fact itself should give us faith that Keynesian ideas can, also, be removed from our political consciousness.

We remain firm in our faith that Americans can shape their own destiny.

Like the Spirit of Christmas Yet to Come, we hope that our conditional predictions will come to be refuted. We hope that our institutions and practices may be reformed in time to prevent "what may be" becoming "what is." Like Robert Frost's traveler, we confront a choice between alternative roads. On the one side, there lies the falsely attractive path toward "national economic planning," a choice that would have us allow government to go beyond traditional bounds because it has failed even to fulfill its more limited promises. On the other side, there is the way of the free society, of men and women living within a constitutional contract that also keeps governments in well-chosen harness. This way, so well understood by Americans two centuries past, has been obscured by the underbrush of burgeoning bureaucracy. Will we, like Robert Frost's traveler, choose the road less traveled?

Indexes

Author Index

Subject Index

This book is set in Minion, a typeface designed by Robert Slimbach specifically for digital typesetting. Released by Adobe in 1989, it is a versatile neohumanist face that shows the influence of Slimbach's own calligraphy.

This book is printed on paper that is acid-free and meets the requirements of the American National Standard for Permanence of Paper for Printed Library Materials, z39.48-1992. ∞

Book design by Louise OFarrell, Gainesville, Fla.
Typography by Impressions Book and Journal Services, Inc., Madison, Wisc.
Printed and bound by Worzalla Publishing Company, Stevens Point, Wisc.